PHOTOHISTORY
of the 20TH
CENTURY

Frontispiece

Ten years after the Vietnam
War ended the suffering
remains. This Vietnamese child
looks at the outside world from
behind the wire fence of the
Bowring refugee camp, one of
Hong Kong's seven Vietnamese
'closed' camps, where almost
6,000 refugees still live as
virtual prisoners.

JONATHAN GRIMWOOD

PHOTOHISTORY
of the 20TH
CENTURY

FOREWORD BY ASA BRIGGS

BLANDFORD PRESS

POOLE · NEW YORK · SYDNEY

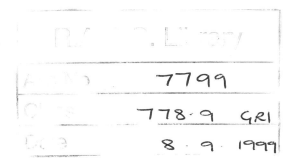
Picture research: Mike Hollingshead, Popperfoto
Picture selection: Mike Hollingshead & Jonathan Grimwood

First published in the UK 1986 by Blandford Press
Link House, West Street, Poole, Dorset BH15 1LL

Distributed in the United States by
Sterling Publishing Co, Inc,
2 Park Avenue, New York, NY 10016

Distributed in Australia by
Capricorn Link (Australia) Pty Ltd
PO Box 665, Lane Cove, NSW 2066

British Library Cataloguing in Publication Data

Grimwood, Jonathan
   Photohistory of the 20th century.
   1. History, Modern—20th Century—Pictorial works
   I. Title
   909.82′022′2   D426

ISBN 0 7137 1802 1

The author and publisher would like
to thank **Mike Hollingshead**, Chief Librarian at
Popperfoto, London for his unstinting help on the picture research.

Typeset by Furlonger Phototext Ltd., Bournemouth
Printed in Great Britain by
BAS Printers Ltd., Wallop, Hampshire

CONTENTS

FOREWORD · *6*   INTRODUCTION · *9*

1901 · *10*   1902 · *11*   1903 · *12*   1904 · *14*   1905 · *15*

1906 · *16*   1907 · *18*   1908 · *19*   1909 · *20*   1910 · *22*   1911 · *24*

1912 · *28*   1913 · *30*   1914 · *32*   1915 · *33*   1916 · *35*   1917 · *38*   1918 · *42*

1919 · *44*   1920 · *45*   1921 · *46*   1922 · *48*   1923 · *50*   1924 · *51*   1925 · *53*   1926 · *54*

1927 · *56*   1928 · *57*   1929 · *58*   1930 · *60*   1931 · *63*   1932 · *65*   1933 · *67*   1934 · *70*   1935 · *71*

1936 · *72*   1937 · *75*   1938 · *77*   1939 · *80*   1940 · *84*   1941 · *88*   1942 · *91*   1943 · *93*

1944 · *96*   1945 · *98*   1946 · *102*   1947 · *103*   1948 · *105*   1949 · *107*   1950 · *108*   1951 · *110*

1952 · *112*   1953 · *114*   1954 · *116*   1955 · *118*   1956 · *119*   1957 · *121*   1958 · *123*

1959 · *125*   1960 · *128*   1961 · *130*   1962 · *133*   1963 · *134*   1964 · *137*   1965 · *138*   1966 · *139*

1967 · *142*   1968 · *145*   1969 · *147*   1970 · *149*   1971 · *151*   1972 · *154*   1973 · *156*

1974 · *157*   1975 · *160*   1976 · *163*   1977 · *166*   1978 · *169*   1979 · *171*

1980 · *174*   1981 · *177*   1982 · *180*   1983 · *184*   1984 · *186*

1985 · *189*   1986 · *191*   INDEX · *192*

FOREWORD

THE AGE OF THE IMAGE

This fascinating collection of twentieth-century photographs, arranged chronologically year by year, should be of interest to both general readers and specialist historians. The visual record of the twentieth century is far more complete than that of any previous century. Indeed, it has been described as the 'age of the image'. As the famous French photographer Gisèle Freund has put it, 'the world is no longer evoked. It is directly represented'.

Many of the images are fleeting. Indeed, it is of the essence of the cinema that film is never still: nonetheless, from the very beginnings of photography, decades before the advent of the cinema, contemporaries asked whether or how it would be possible to use the camera to document history. Many answers have been given. There would be agreement now, however, that while the fleeting images of film and television can provide access to the past, still photographs are essential evidence, especially for the pre-television years. Moreover, their subject range is far wider than that of the cinema.

All the photographs in this book, varied indeed though they are in subject and style, come from one remarkable archive — the libraries of Popperfoto — one of a number of important international archives. The primary function of Popperfoto is to make particular photographs speedily available for reproduction to publishers, television and the press throughout the world: yet as this book demonstrates, such photographs, when assembled together, provide a mass of historical evidence to set alongside other kinds of evidence — documentary, statistical, architectural and cultural.

These photographs come from all parts of the world: indeed, they reveal how different parts of the world have figured in relation to the rest — and they have figured very differently — at different times during the twentieth century.

The great archives of the nineteenth century were archives of manuscripts and books. It was the words that mattered, and when they were made available they were subjected to intense examination. By the end of the century, however, both the typewriter and, more important, the telephone were beginning to change the nature of such archives. It was then also that the first photographic libraries began to be assembled — at first often on a very small scale. Popperfoto's own collection incorporates among others the earlier Paul Popper library (which included such material as the photographs taken by Herbert Ponting on the 1910-1912 Scott Antarctic expedition), and the Odhams Periodicals Library which included the complete files of more than fifty journals ranging from *The Passing Show* to *Women's Realm*.

Photographs as evidence need to be interpreted as carefully and as critically as documents or biographies or buildings: it is a serious mistake to take photographs for granted as being 'true', more true than words which can lie. How photographs are made, why and for whom are just as relevant and interesting questions as when they are made. Like films they are not 'unadulterated reflections of historical truth'. By their nature they select: by design they can distort.

In retrospect we can often discern elements of propaganda which were not apparent at the time. There has, of course, been a direct use of photographs for propaganda purposes in this century in the same way that paintings — or statues — were sometimes used for propaganda in previous centuries.

Further considerations affect interpretation. Photography itself has changed radically during this century not only in its equipment, its techniques and its styles but in its organisation and its context. 'Gentleman artists' have not disappeared from the ranks of photographers, but new types of professional photographs have emerged, producing quickly accessible and usable images often in the form of pictorial journalism as represented, for example, by *Illustrated*, one of the magazines in the Popperfoto collection.

The first of such magazines, the *Berliner Illustrierte* and the *Müncher Illustrierte Presse* of the 1920s, focussed attention on the subject matter of the photograph, as did *Vu* magazine in Paris, founded in 1928, or *Life* magazine in the United States, founded in 1936.

'From any place where important events occur,' ran the first editorial in *Vu*, 'photographs . . . will reach *Vu*, linking our readership with the entire world . . . and bringing the universality of life to the eye'.

'To see life; to see the world . . . to watch the faces of the poor and the gestures of the proud' were the first declared objects of the first number of *Life*, which went on to add other items like 'to see strange things — machines, armies, multitudes, shadows in the jungle and on the moon'.

The most important object of all, it was claimed, was 'to see and to take pleasure in seeing; to see and be amazed; to see and be instructed'. It might have added 'to see and become concerned', for that was an object which was to inspire 'photostories', a new form of photographic presentation, and which was to pass from the Press into television.

Meanwhile, the rise of popular photography, recorded in thousands of family snapshot albums, further multiplied the number of extant images, and the Japanese both as manufacturers and as users of cameras have come to figure as prominently in the twentieth-century image story as the Americans, the Germans, the French or the British. The camera has served effectively as a private as well as a public instrument, as Brian Coe and Paul Gates showed in their pioneering study *The Snapshot Photograph* (1977), which takes the story only as far as 1939, long before the invention of the Instamatic. It reveals throughout, however, how family pictures can be just as valuable evidence for the historian as pictorial journalism or campaign photographs. There has always been a further category of photographs also — publicity pictures, some of them for advertising purposes — and these, too, have their historical uses. They can illuminate a whole culture.

There are many different kinds of photographs shown in this photohistory of the twentieth century, which has some of the characteristics of our family snapshot album: some of the photographs present news in the making, others what lay behind the news: and most pictures tell a story, many of them without the help of the captions.

A number of the pictures are concerned with social history. These deal with ways of life, some of them lost ways, not with great events, and with people whose names have been forgotten — not with names in the history books or, for that matter, in the newspapers of the time. There are many contrasts in here. It is interesting to compare, for example, the 1907 photograph of members of the Russian royal family along with King Edward VII and Queen Alexandra and the 1908 photograph of a group of holidaymakers at Margate.

There is more about 'pop culture' (or 'mass culture') than about 'high culture' in the collection, itself a sign of the times; although Tolstoy is shown in his study in 1910 and Nureyev, significantly not on the stage but at a press conference, in 1961. Film, such an ubiquitous force in pop culture, is represented, like sport, in many pictures, including the 1920 scene of Charlie Chaplin in *The Kid*; the photographs of Greta Garbo in 1926, Shirley Temple in 1938 and Clark Gable and Vivien Leigh in 1939; and the photographs of James Dean in 1955 and of Elvis Presley in 1960. The sounds of music, indeed, often burst through. So, too, do the voices of the taste-makers. Fashion photographs are a genre in themselves, and although there are only a few of them in this collection, the 1924 photograph of a mannequin should be compared with the 1950 Christian Dior picture. How and why fashions change are key questions for social and cultural historians.

'Nature', which itself has changed in a century of change, figures in the background of many of the pictures of people and of buildings. There are more direct pictures of 'natural disasters', however, a staple of the Press, and also an extremely striking 1977 photograph of a fire-gutted warehouse in Minneapolis which was turned into a palace of icicles as tons of water from the firemen's hoses froze in the winter cold. Striking in a different way is the 1911 photograph by Harold Ponting of a grotto in an iceberg in Antarctica — a part of the world now once again in the news. From a later date Mount St Helens in Washington State is shown erupting in 1980, sending a cloud of steam and ash 60,000 feet in the air.

The 1965 balloon view of the Alps taken with a camera with a fish-eye lens is in line with a tradition of views from the air — of cities as well as of landscapes. The moon, however, is a recent 'discovery', and there is a 1963 picture of the world's first space woman, Valentina Tereshkova, in this collection. The Russians had launched the first artificial satellite in 1957, and in 1969 American astronauts landed on the moon, another key picture of what was far more than a media event. Photographs of 'the other side of the moon' had been taken in 1957, and 15,000 high resolution photographs of the moon's surface had been recorded by Rangers 7, 8 and 9 in 1964 and 1965.

Our sense of Nature has changed profoundly during the course of this century largely because of developments in the sciences, particularly physics, followed by the biological sciences: they have set out not only to understand Nature but to make use of its secrets. The 1945 bomb on Hiroshima, one of the most famous of pictures, can be set alongside the first heart transplant of 1967. In both cases scientific discovery is carrying with it complex chains of human consequences. Most of the photographs in this collection demonstrate, however, that much about men and women has not changed in a century of change: despite all the weight of specific and dated content in the particular photographs of any particular year, there are recurring human themes to set alongside natural disaster — appalling suffering; the weight of pomp and ceremony; the violence of popular revolt. *Plus ça change, plus c'est la même chose.* One of the most haunting pictures is the 1963 suicide of a Buddhist priest in Vietnam, not unique however, but the fifth of such ritual suicides. And Vietnam still figures in the most recent 1985 photographs — along with Ethiopia.

While some of such pictures need no captions, most do; and it should be noted that in the course of this century the same picture — given different captions — has often carried with it different and even opposed messages. The captions in this volume are strictly factual: they are designed to place the pictures in their context, not to 'interpret' them.

Asa Briggs
Worcester College, Oxford

INTRODUCTION

For almost all of history, the *majority* of people — whatever or wherever their civilisations — believed that the situation around them was stable and lasting; that society was then as it would be until the world ended, that nothing would change.

Ours, however, is a century which has seen the world change almost beyond recognition. A great deal of the change that we have seen, we have indeed *seen* because it has been recorded by the camera. And yet, as Asa Briggs points out in his foreword, photographs are not 'unadulterated reflections of historical truth'. By their nature they select, by design they can distort: which is why the captions in this book are factual, designed to place the pictures in context, not to 'interpret' them.

1901 — 1914: An End To The Old Order. By the turn of the century, the camera had already given to many something once reserved for the well-to-do — 'portraits' of themselves and of their families. Artificial in pose though these early photographs were, they instilled a sense of belonging: and it is one of the minor ironies of history that they reached the height of their popularity at a point when the extended family was once again about to decline.

At the turn of the century, newspapers and magazines received their news via the telegraph, but still relied on artists to supply pictures to back up the stories. This was to alter with the development of press photography; and one of the first results was that it became more difficult — though by no means impossible — for magazines and newspapers to present war or deprivation visually in a glamorous light. It is easier to instruct an artist to produce a sketch of outstanding heroism or picturesque poverty than it is to order a photographer to find such an event and photograph it. This left an option of staging such pictures, which happened often, but which in the long term was self-defeating because such fakery tended to show.

Another important result of early press photography was that ways of life that had been foreign became less so; and although this was initially treated as an opportunity for exoticism (see the photograph on p16 of the Ottoman harem girl), it meant that cultures began to move more rapidly towards each other. So much so that by the late 20th century, under the influence of television, film, video and the international press, large areas of the world's popular culture had become homogenised.

But for most of the western world in the early years between the beginning of the century and the coming of the Great War, life still seemed ordered, and despite Marconi's revolutionary trans-Atlantic wireless transmission (p10), the first-ever powered flight, by the Wright brothers (p13) and the rise of the Suffragette movement (p20 & p30), all of which were to have a major effect on the coming century, the future still seemed predictable.

English hop pickers in East Kent, in the year of Queen Victoria's death. Although the work was hard, the migration of whole communities from London to the hop fields allowed families to breathe fresh air away from the streets of the major city: and many families regarded it as a working 'holiday'.

Several eminent scientists had stated that the curvature of the earth would limit telegraphy to about 200 miles, but on 12 December the first *transatlantic* wireless transmissions were received on this equipment, set up on Signal Hill, St John's, Newfoundland by the inventor of wireless telegraphy, Guglielmo Marconi (1874-1937). Marconi, who poses here by the receiver that picked up those first morse signals from Cornwall, in the southwest of England, later shared the Nobel Prize for Physics (in 1909). His invention was to revolutionise the gathering and dispersal of international news.

Edward VII (1841-1910) stands in the regalia of a high-ranking freemason, his hand upon the 'book of worship'. Edward VII came to the throne of Great Britain upon the death of Queen Victoria and was crowned in the following year. As Prince of Wales he had been Grand Master of the English Freemasons, a title inherited by his son, the Duke of York, later King George VI. Freemasonry — which first appeared as a ritual brotherhood in 17th-century England — quickly became, throughout Britain, America and the Protestant world the preserve of the wealthy and respectable middle classes; it also became part of the cement binding together the British Empire and many Indian princes were admitted to membership.

1903

Efficient and modern, the Krupp armaments factory built in 1903 at Essen on the River Ruhr, where the family already owned one of the world's largest steelworks. This new factory supplied the Imperial German forces with their munitions during the build up to and throughout World War I; and later rearmed Nazi Germany in the run up to World War II.

Indian officials and British dignitaries gather for the opening of the Mayurbhani State Railway. Everywhere the British went in the days of their Empire, they built a railway. In India especially, the railway imposed upon the continent a unity it had not seen before, linking together communities that had always been separate. The process of railway building throughout the British Empire was a continuous one that went on long after the great period of railway expansion in Britain and America had ended.

大清國當今聖母皇太后萬歲萬歲萬歲

The Manchu Empress Tz'u Hi (1834-1908), who ruled China for fifty years, flanked by ladies of her court. She vigorously opposed modernisation of the country and supported the ill-fated Boxer Rebellion of 1900, which she saw as a tool to drive all foreigners from China. When the Rebellion was put down by an international force and Peking captured, Tz'u Hi tried to save herself and her dynasty with a belated programme of reform, but the fall of the Manchu dynasty was postponed only until 1911, when the last emperor of China, 5-year-old Pu Yi, was deposed and China became a republic.

'No Balloon Attached', announced an American newspaper in amazement. Orville Wright makes the first flight, at Kitty Hawk, North Carolina, on 17 December in *Flyer I*, the first airplane to achieve powered, sustained and piloted flight. Designed and built by the Wright brothers, Wilbur (1867-1912) and Orville (1871-1948), the *Flyer* made four flights on that day, the first of which lasted 12 seconds and the longest of which covered a ground distance of 852 feet (230 metres) and lasted 59 seconds!

A pair of Tsarist soldiers bound to the stake by two Japanese infantrymen who are dressed in copies of European military uniform and carry rifles. Japan — unwisely regarded by Europe as an archaic, minor Asiatic power — faced Russia and destroyed the myth of European military supremacy with devastating thoroughness.

Two relief ships, *Morning* and *Terra Nova* — seen here in the McMurdo Strait, Antarctica on 5 January. Robert Falcon Scott (1868-1912), a Royal Navy commander, led the National Antarctic Expedition which in 1901-4 explored the Ross Sea area of Antarctica in a specially prepared research ship, *Discovery* — and launched a decade of intensive overland Antarctic exploration, which for Scott was to end in death, following his failure to be first to the South Pole.

The Russian cruiser *Bayan* lies peacefully at anchor at Port Arthur, a Chinese port used as a naval base by the Russians. In February a squadron of Japanese ships under Admiral Togo launched a surprise attack on the Russian fleet at Port Arthur, and triggered the Russo-Japanese War. Nearly 40 years later the Japanese attack on an unsuspecting Pearl Harbor was to bring America into World War II.

Leo Tolstoy (1828-1910) at work in his study at Yasnaya Polyana. His greatest and best-known works were by this time long behind him. *War and Peace*, the epic novel of Russian society during the Napoleonic Wars, had been finished in 1869 and the poignant love story *Anna Karenina* in 1877.

At a time when other monarchies were in the process of dissolution, Norway was re-establishing itself as an independent kingdom. When Norway dissolved its union with Sweden in June 1905, the Norwegian throne was offered to Prince Charles of Denmark who, as Haakon VII (1872-1952), ruled Norway until his death. He married Maud, the youngest daughter of King Edward VII of England, and their son Harald became the first heir-presumptive to be born in the country since 1370.

A Russian gun captured by the Japanese during the Russo-Japanese War, on exhibition in Tokyo. Japanese victories over Russia at sea and on land (in Korea and Manchuria), which put paid to Tsarist Russia's expansionist ambitions in the Far East, also fuelled Japan's ambition to become a major world power.

Tin miners at the Dalcoath mine in Cornwall break from work to enjoy traditional miners' fare, the Cornish pasty — one of the earliest pre-packaged convenience foods.

A woman of a Turkish harem. Under the Ottoman Empire, Turkey, after a flirtation with constitutional and social reform in the second half of the 19th century, had reverted to stagnation and tyranny by the early 1900s. But the Young Turks — a group of progressive army officers — were pressing for a programme of modernisation and by 1908 forced the Sultan to convene a parliament.

Opposite: The ruins of the City Hall of San Francisco after earthquake devastated the city at 5.15 in the morning on 18 April. In the three-day fire that followed the earthquake over 500 people died, 250,000 were left homeless and more than four square miles of the city were destroyed. Reports of the disaster were received by American newspapers over the telegraph, enabling the story to appear in some of that day's papers.

Opposite: Heavily retouched though it is, this is one of the world's earliest on-the-spot news photographs, and also one of the most expensive, commanding a £100 reproduction fee in 1906. Taken only moments after an attempt to assassinate King Alfonso XIII of Spain (1886-1941) in May, it shows the chaos that followed when an anarchist bomb exploded near the coach in which Alfonso and his bride, Eugenia of Battenberg, were returning from their wedding in Madrid. The king escaped injury and lived to survive four more assassination attempts.

Rudyard Kipling (1865-1936), the writer whose stories were meant to epitomise the spirit of the British Raj — 1907 was a year after the publication of *Puck of Pook's Hill*, and the year in which he was awarded the Nobel Prize for Literature. Kipling had in 1895 refused to become Britain's Poet Laureate; later he three times declined the Order of Merit and refused a knighthood, holding that writers should be free from restrictions imposed by state honours.

Hailed in the 1900s as one of the new century's greatest living sculptors, the Norwegian Gustav Vigeland (1869-1943) upset the art world with his series of nudes in granite and bronze. Here, in a detail from a sequence from 1907 onwards, a pubescent girl falls through the branches of the 'tree of life'. He studied in Berlin where Expressionism was at its height.

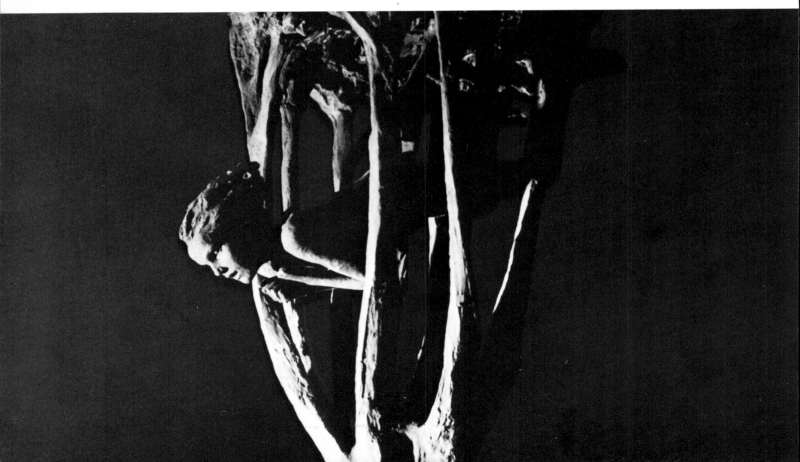

Tsar Nicholas II, his family and that of his cousin, Edward VII. Queen Alexandra (left: then standing) Princess Ingeborg of Denmark; Duchess of Oldenburg (Tsar's sister); Tsarina Alexandra; Princess Victoria; Tsar; Edward VII; Queen of Norway; Prince Harald of Denmark; King of Norway; Queen and King of Denmark. The Tsar's daughters (left) were to die with their parents nine years later.

The Italian runner Dorando Pietri, first man to finish the London Olympic marathon, staggers across the line. For two hours he was close to death. He was disqualified for receiving medical help on the track after entering the stadium, to run the last lap on the point of collapse, but recovered to receive a gold cup as consolation from Queen Alexandra.

A group of holidaymakers at the British seaside resort of Margate. Reductions in working hours and increases in real earnings made holidays possible for many working people early this century and seaside resorts grew to cater to this new market.

1909

The Frenchman Louis Blériot (1872-1936) wins, in a monoplane of his own design, the race to be the first to fly across the English Channel, on 25 July. He flew from Les Baraques in France to a field near Dover Castle in Kent.

The Suffragette Movement in Britain became more active and more militant after 1906, when its leaders failed to persuade the Liberal party to adopt women's suffrage as part of its policy. Publicity stunts were many and varied. Muriel Manners, who had already created news by chaining herself to the grill of the Ladies' Gallery while attempting to make a speech to Parliament, flew over the House shouting 'Votes for Women' through a megaphone.

Opposite: The Niagara Falls frozen solid during the exceptionally severe winter of 1909.

The election which lost the Lords much of their power. A Liberal candidate in Kent points to his campaign message. The January election was fought on the issue of the People's Budget, introduced by the Liberal chancellor of the exchequer, David Lloyd George (1863-1945), in the previous year. This had provided for super-tax and was thrown out by the House of Lords. The Conservative answer was Tariff Reform. The Lords' power was reduced by the Parliament Act of 1911.

King Edward VII died in May. In the funeral procession, here passing beneath the walls of Windsor Castle, the new king, George V (1865-1936), is attended by his sons the Prince of Wales and Prince Albert and by his nephew Kaiser Wilhelm II of Germany.

A rail hand-car negotiates a steep and rugged section of the Transandine Railway, which was opened on 5 April. The line — between Valparaiso, Chile, and Mendoza, Argentina — was almost 900 miles long and climbed to an altitude of 10,466 feet (3,191 metres) at its highest point, the La Cumbre tunnel.

The Death's Head Hussars, an elite force of the German army, drawn up for inspection by the Crown Prince Wilhelm. The growing strength of the German army and, particularly, navy at this period was an ominous sign of Imperial Germany's expansionist *Weltpolitik*.

The men's moustaches and the women's hats and high-necked dresses give the game away — these two groups are recognisably from the same milieu. They inhabit neither the same continent nor the same culture, but these two middle-class families — one in Croydon, England, the other in Istanbul, Turkey — share a common life style and a common outlook. World War I was to shatter this self-assurance, bringing revolution to Turkey, a slow but inexorable end of empire to Britain and an end to the seemingly endless extended family.

The British home secretary, Winston Churchill (1874-1965), watches from the cover of a gateway at the 'siege of Sidney Street', 3 January. Churchill brought in the Scots Guards against two armed anarchists holed up in a house in London's East End. This was the year that newspapers claimed there was a 'suffragette plot' to kidnap the home secretary.

Opposite: George V poses in full panoply with his Queen, Mary, after his coronation on 22 June as King of Great Britain and Emperor of India. He was without political experience and his reign was not to be as untroubled, or as secure as this confident State photograph suggests; it was marked by World War I, by industrial unrest and economic depression.

This superb picture of a grotto in an iceberg was taken by Herbert Ponting (1870-1935), one of the greatest photographers of Antarctica. As 'camera artist', Ponting accompanied Scott on his ill-fated second expedition to the South Pole which, at the time this photograph was taken, in 1911, had established its base on McMurdo Sound.

Opposite: In an almost informal photograph the 39-year-old Norwegian explorer Roald Amundsen (1872-1928) stands at the South Pole. He reached this on 14 December, while Scott's party, having dispensed with its dog teams, was still struggling to haul its heavy sledges through the soft snow above the Ross Ice Shelf. The race for the Pole and the exploration of Antarctica was a matter of great concern for the British Empire, and news of Amundsen's victory was a bitter blow to national pride.

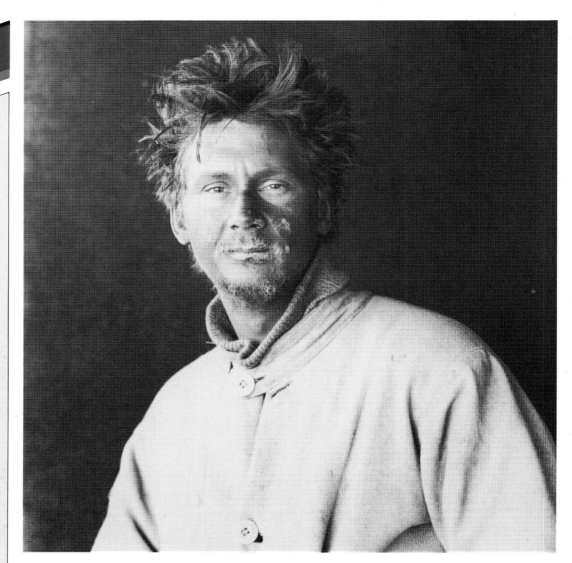

Charles Seymour Wright (b1887) was the physicist to Scott's expedition and was a member of one of the support parties for the final march to the Pole. Frostbite and exhaustion mask his face in this photograph taken (by Herbert Ponting) on his return to base camp, 29 January.

Captain Scott's party posed for a photograph at the South Pole, which they reached on 17 January – a month after Amundsen. Sick with disappointment, Scott wrote in his diary that day, 'This is an awful place and terrible enough for us to have laboured to it without the reward of priority.' This picture was developed from a negative found after Scott's death by a party from base camp who had gone to search for the party's remains.

Opposite: Cheerful passengers wave farewell from the decks of the White Star liner *Titanic*, newest, biggest and best of the transatlantic liners, as she leaves Southampton on her maiden voyage.

Opposite: Halfway across the Atlantic, at 10.20 at night on 14 April, the 'unsinkable' *Titanic* struck an iceberg and sank within four hours with the loss of 1,513 lives. A fleet of rescue ships, summoned by wireless, arrived after she had sunk but in time to save 732 survivors, like these two boatloads photographed arriving alongside the *Carpathian*. First indication of the disaster was when the Marconi wireless station in Newfoundland picked up the *Titanic's* distress signals.

1913

The launch at Portsmouth, 16 October, of Britain's first oil-powered Dreadnought, HMS *Queen Elizabeth*. The Dreadnoughts — big, fast, heavily-gunned battleships — were the spearheads and symbols of the pre-World War I naval armaments race. The fear that Germany might end up with more Dreadnoughts than Britain inflamed British public opinion and forced the government to build more and more of these great ships.

Death at the Derby, 4 June, as the suffragette Emily Davidson hurls herself under the hooves of the King's horse at Tattenham Corner.

Opposite: Kaiser Wilhelm II of Germany riding with his cousin George V of Britain outside the old Hohenzollern palace at Potsdam, near Berlin. In a little over a year their two countries would be at war. This was a family occasion, George V having come to Germany for the wedding of the Kaiser's daughter.

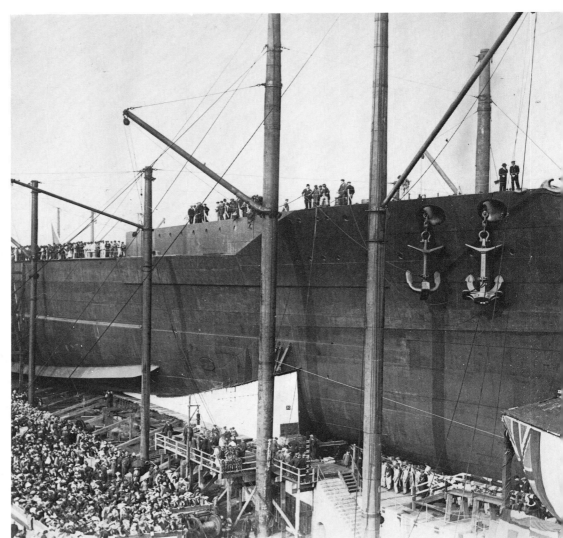

1914

The SS *Ancon*, the first ship to pass through the Panama Canal on its opening day, 15 August. The Canal, fifty miles long, saved vessels a long and dangerous voyage of 6,000 miles around the tip of South America and gave America — who controlled the Canal Zone under treaty — a firm foothold in Central America.

The Archduke Francis Ferdinand (1863-1914), heir to the Austrian throne, and his wife leave the town hall of Sarajevo, 28 June. A matter of minutes later they had both been shot dead and the train of diplomatic events that led within six weeks to the start of World War I had been set in motion. Sarajevo was the capital of Bosnia, which had recently been annexed by Austria. The Austrians believed that Serbia was behind the outrage and declared war. A series of treaties then brought all the major powers into the war on one side or on the other.

Romance and unreality: a young volunteer in the Austro-Hungarian army poses for the camera before leaving for the Eastern Front to fight in a war that would eventually destroy the Empire for which he fought. Smart though his uniform was, it was desperately unsuited to the hard realities of war.

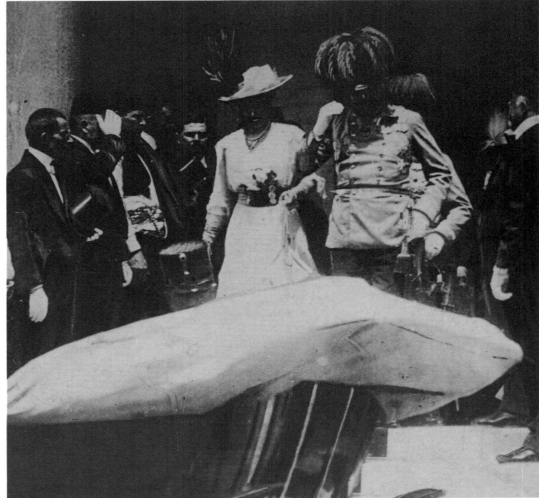

1915 — 1927: Over The Great Divide. The war, on a scale not seen before, that started between the imperial powers of Europe, their worldwide empires and their allies in 1914, and which involved America from 1917 (p38), was to divide politically, technically and intellectually what had gone before from what came after. Despite this, the war was not unexpected. Indeed it was a possibility for which many of the participants — especially Germany and Britain — had been busily preparing (p23 & p30).

The change that the conflict and its aftermath brought to science, attitudes and the political shape of the world was enormous, and lasting. By the end of the war, the aeroplane — only developed in the previous decade and initially used in the conflict only for reconnaissance — had taken battle upwards into a third dimension: meanwhile the tank had evolved from Kitchener's 'pretty mechanical toy' into a major land weapon: one which, along with the armoured car, was to render cavalry obsolete.

Not all developments were military. Lessons learned in the air, which at first led in the following decade to the great age of air exploration with Alan Cobham's first flight to Australia and back in 1926 (p54) and Charles Lindbergh's even more famous solo flight in 1927 across the Atlantic (p56), eventually resulted in an age of air travel, which shrank the world even further.

Nor was it surprising if art, manners and morals became freer in the aftermath of a war which saw the fall of Europe's great imperial families and the break-up of their huge and formal empires. The Romanovs of Russia, the Hohenzollerns of Germany, the Hapsburgs of Austria-Hungary, the Sublime Porte of the Ottoman Empire: all were swept from power, along with dozens of minor royal and princely families.

The age of Jazz was being born, of film idols and popular heroes. It was a time of both F. Scott Fitzgerald's *This Side of Paradise* and T. S. Eliot's *The Waste Land* (1920 and 1922 respectively). And for a while after the war it seemed that Japan might remain a staunch Far Eastern ally to Britain and America, that India could possibly remain, with Australia, New Zealand and Canada, comfortably within the British Empire, and that the newly created states of Europe would join in establishing a great and lasting democratic age under the benign influence of the League of Nations.

1915

The last moments of the German battle-cruiser *Blucher*, sunk on 28 January in the Battle of the Dogger Bank, between a German squadron reconnoitring in the North Sea and a British battle-cruiser squadron under Sir David Beatty (1871-1936). The photograph was taken by a sailor on the deck of a British cruiser.

Allied positions at 'Anzac' Cove on the Gallipoli peninsula, heavily fortified against Turkish assaults. For eight months Australian, New Zealand and British troops held a precarious toe-hold on the peninsula; they were withdrawn after suffering 100,000 casualties. The Gallipoli disaster cost Winston Churchill, the expedition's foremost champion in London, his job as First Lord of the Admiralty.

Christmas — and troops in a village in the Russian sector of war-torn Poland take time out of the conflict to decorate their Christmas tree with candles.

In Mexico several years of political chaos followed the forced resignation in 1911 of Head of State Portifiro Diaz, as the country split into warring factions. One faction was headed by Pancho Villa (1877-1923), the Mexican bandit and revolutionary general who, by the time this photograph was taken, had become a virtual dictator, with the whole of northern Mexico under his control. He made his peace with the Mexican government in 1920 and retired to his ranch where, in 1923, he was murdered by his secretary.

British soldiers man the barricades in Dublin during the Easter Rising of April, when Irish Republicans proclaimed an independent Irish Republic, issuing orders from the General Post Office, which they used as their headquarters during the fighting. The uprising — which was initially unpopular with the people of Dublin — was suppressed after a week of bitter fighting. By executing 14 of the leaders, the British ensured that the rising would not be forgotten and would pass into legend.

Grigory Rasputin (1871-1916), the Russian monk and mystic whose power over the Tsarina gave him an enormous influence in Russian politics, at a genteel tea party with some of his admirers. He was widely believed to be in the pay of the Germans and was soon, in December, to be assassinated.

A photographer on a British destroyer caught this shot of near-misses falling alongside a German warship during the Battle of Jutland, 31 May-1 June. Jutland was the only occasion during World War I in which the main German and British battle fleets — for which both countries had clamoured for so long — met in battle. Inconclusive though it was, it dissuaded the German fleet from venturing on the high seas for the rest of the war.

Opposite: As this photograph shows, there was precious little romance or glamour left by 1916 for the soldiers enduring trench warfare on the Western Front. During the Battle of the Somme, the biggest offensive mounted up to then by the Allies which started in July, 20,000 British soldiers were killed on the first day alone of the infantry assault. By 18 November between them the armies had lost 1,250,000 killed or wounded. An exhausted, wounded German prisoner-of-war photographed as he is escorted from the front-line mud by a British military policeman during the Battle of the Ancre, November. Behind him is another photographer.

1917

American troops being welcomed at a British seaport. The United States declared war on Germany on 6 April and American troops were rushed to the Western Front: by the end of the war there were over a million in France. Their arrival gave a necessary boost to Allied morale.

'A pretty mechanical toy' was how General Kitchener (1850-1916) described the tank, and tanks (used first by the British in 1916) at first floundered uselessly in the battlefield mud: but they soon became practical instruments of war — like this early model traversing a trench on the Western Front in April.

Opposite: Under arrest in Siberia, Nicholas II, once Tsar of all Russia and commander-in-chief of the Russian army, waits at Tsarskoe Selo after abdicating in March 1917. The news of his execution haunted, ever after, his cousin and friend George V of Britain.

Conscription, which took millions of working people away from the factories and herded them into the armed forces, left Britain with an immense shortage of labour. The gap was filled at least partly by women, who took over men's jobs in workshops, on the land and even, as here, on the buses. The suffragettes abandoned their demonstrations for the duration, demanding instead the 'right to serve'. Having proved their usefulness and their power, women over 30 who fulfilled the right property qualifications were 'rewarded' with the vote in 1918; votes for women between 21 and 30 were not granted until 1928.

Opposite: Passchendaele. This village was the furthest point reached by Allied troops in the Third Battle of Ypres, when it was captured by Canadian troops on 9 November. The offensive coincided with the heaviest rain in the area for thirty years, which turned the battleground into such a swamp that it took twelve men, wading waist-deep in the sludge, to carry to safety one wounded man on a stretcher. The name Passchendaele became to the British and Canadians what Verdun was to the French — a symbol of the War's horror.

Opposite: The new Bolshevik regime in Russia offered the German High Command an armistice, which was signed on 15 December; here a blindfolded Russian envoy is escorted to German army headquarters during the negotiations.

The 'Red Baron', Manfred von Richtofen, the greatest German fighter-pilot 'ace' of World War I, who was killed in action on 21 April.

Marshal Ferdinand Foch (1857-1929), Supreme Allied Commander on the Western Front (second from right), leaving the railway coach at Compiègne in which, on 11 November, he had signed the armistice that ended the slaughter of World War I — 'at the eleventh hour of the eleventh day of the eleventh month'. Hitler was later to demand of the French that their surrender early in World War II be signed in the same carriage.

The war is over! British soldiers on the Western Front — these are men of the 9th East Surreys — cheer the news of the armistice.

Opposite: Conscription had been introduced in Britain in 1916, but only in 1918 did the British government propose to extend it to Ireland. The opposition was immediate and vehement. Anti-conscription posters like this appeared all over Dublin; Roman Catholic congregations pledged themselves to resist conscription; and on 23 April a general strike closed down all Ireland.

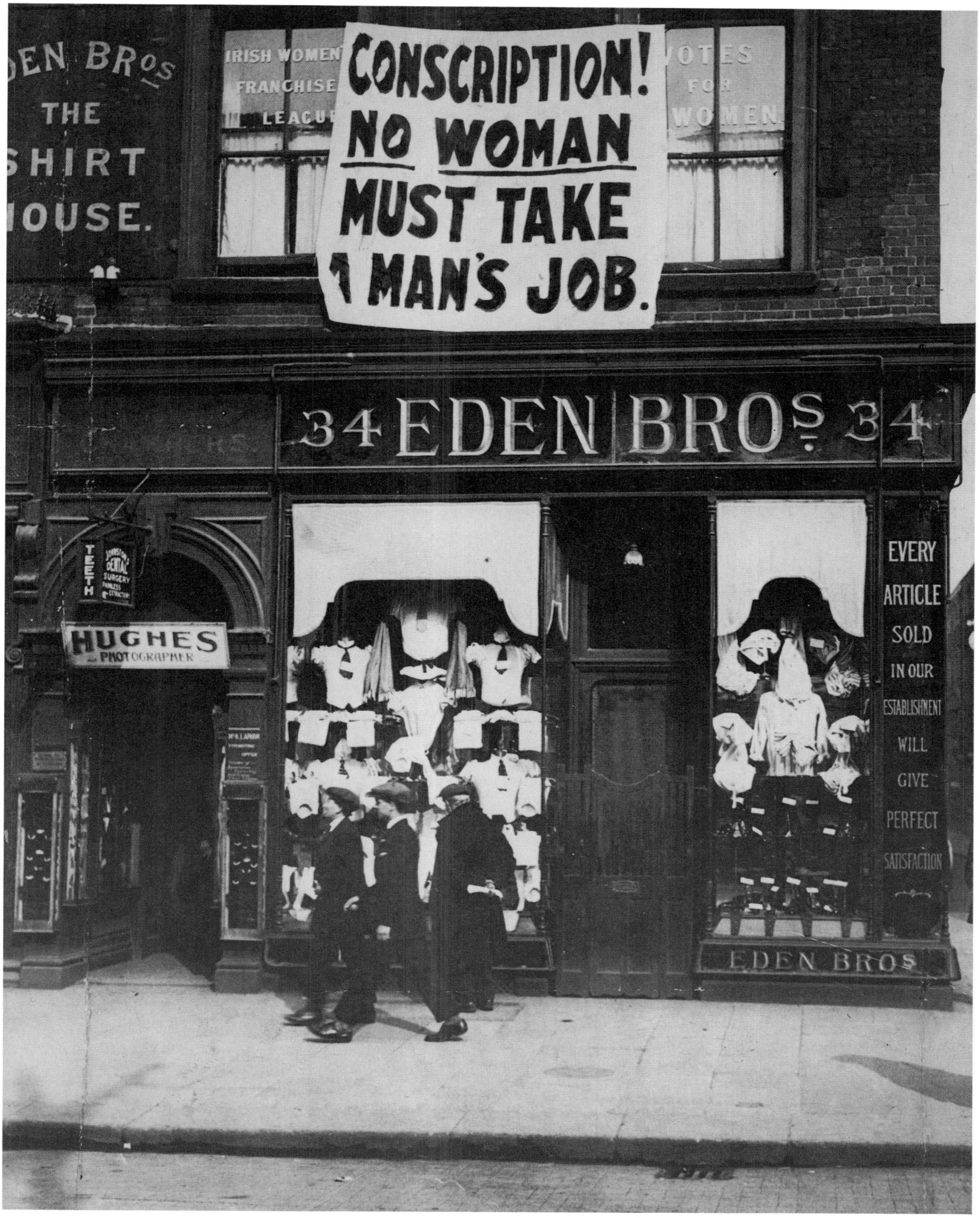
DEN BROS
THE
SHIRT
OUSE.
IRISH WOMEN
FRANCHISE
LEAGU
CONSCRIPTION!
NO WOMAN
MUST TAKE
A MAN'S JOB.
OTES
FOR
WOMEN
34 EDEN BROS 34
TEETH
HUGHES
PHOTOGRAPHER
EVERY
ARTICLE
SOLD
IN OUR
ESTABLISHMENT
WILL
GIVE
PERFECT
SATISFACTION
EDEN BROS

1919

United States President Woodrow Wilson (1856-1924) leads the French Prime Minister Georges Clemenceau (1841-1929) and the British Foreign Secretary Arthur Balfour (1848-1930) on a visit to Versailles to see that arrangements are complete for the signing — a few days later, on 28 June — of the peace treaty that formed the basis of the post-war settlement imposed by the victorious Allies.

Officers of the British airship R34 (one of them, second from left, wearing a borrowed American tunic) pose for a photograph at Mineola, Long Island, after making the first airship crossing of the Atlantic, 2-6 July. R34, the largest airship in the world, successfully made the return crossing a few days later. Ten years later the Germans achieved the first round the world flight with the *Graf Zeppelin*.

Nancy Astor (1879-1964), the American-born British Member of Parliament who became, on 1 December, the first woman to take a seat in the House of Commons, a year after women had first been given the vote. A champion of women's rights, she had been an influential political hostess before 'succeeding' her husband as MP for Plymouth.

Charlie Chaplin (1889-1977), who had been a music hall comedian, with child star Jackie Coogan (b1914) in a scene from Chaplin's first feature-length film, *The Kid,* a crime-comedy released in 1920. Film was to become a major means of communication and influence in the 1920s and of escape in the 1930s when it provided refuge from the hardship of the Depression.

Baron Fisher (1841-1920), the British admiral who was the architect and inspirer of the modernisation of the Royal Navy in preparation for World War I, died in 1920. A difficult and outspoken man, he had retired in 1910, been recalled as First Sea Lord by Winston Churchill in 1914 and retired again in 1915. He had been chiefly responsible for Britain's superiority over Germany in the number of Dreadnoughts she had ready for sea at the beginning of the war.

British troops and armoured cars in Dublin during the Anglo-Irish War of 1919-1921, when the Irish Republican Army took on the British forces in a fierce guerilla war. The violence culminated in 'Bloody Sunday', 21 November, with many Englishmen shot dead by the IRA on the streets of Dublin and the Black and Tans — special reinforcements recruited by the British to the Royal Irish Constabulary — retaliating by opening fire on crowds at a football match. The 'Irish Free State' was created in 1922.

Henri Landru (1869-1922), the 'French Bluebeard', sits stoically awaiting the verdict after his widely publicised trial in November. He was convicted of the murders of ten women and a boy, in spite of the fact that none of the bodies were ever found, and was guillotined.

The United States went dry in January when the 18th Amendment to the Constitution banned the manufacture, sale or carriage of *all* alcoholic drinks. Throughout the 1920s prohibition was widely evaded. Like Communism, wrote the humorist Will Rogers in 1927, 'It's a good idea, but it won't work'. In this 1921 photograph, taken in New York, state troopers confiscate a load of bootleg liquor.

Opposite: The original terms for the Treaty of Versailles included abolition of the German airforce and U-boats, massive reduction of the army and navy, colonies to be handed over and over £5,000,000,000 to be paid in compensation. They also provided that the German Rhineland should be occupied for fifteen years by Allied troops. Here, in May, French soldiers of the occupying force set up a machine gun beneath the statue of the great German poet Schiller in Frankfurt-on-Main.

1922

Fascist troops in Rome, October. Following some success in the polls and violence in the streets, their leader, Benito Mussolini (1883-1945), who was in Milan, was invited by the Italian King Victor Emmanuel III — who wanted to avoid civil war — to come to the capital to form a government. These events later became enshrined in Fascist mythology as 'the March on Rome', but the reality was less dramatic: Mussolini came by train, as did most of his followers, and the marching was purely ceremonial.

David Lloyd George, known only half jokingly as 'the Welsh Wizard', trying his hand at water divining. 1922 was to be his last year as British prime minister.

Archaeologist Howard Carter (1873-1939) and his backer Lord Carnarvon outside the steps leading to the 'magnificent tomb with seals intact' discovered by Carter on 6 November. The tomb turned out to be that of the young pharaoh Tutankhamun: the treasures it contained remained untouched – exactly as they had been left nearly 3,500 years before.

Éamonn De Valéra (1882-1975), President of Sinn Féin, reviewing a contingent of the Irish Republican Army in 1922. De Valera and the IRA soon parted company. He went on to build up the Fianna Fáil party and became, at its head, prime minister of the Irish Free State in 1932, and then the first prime minister of Eire.

1923

The Weimar Republic, from its beginning in 1919, existed in a condition of permanent political and economic crisis as it tried to cope with the aftermath of defeat and with crippling war reparations. Spiralling inflation peaked in 1923, when the German mark became quite literally not worth the paper it was printed on. Here clerks use wicker hampers to collect from a Berlin bank the money needed to pay their firm's wages.

French troops in the Ruhr in January. France occupied the Ruhr, Germany's chief industrial and mining region, when Germany proved unable to keep up the payments to France demanded as war reparations.

Tokyo was struck by a massive earthquake on 1 September. Some 140,000 people died and about eight square miles of the city, including the business section (shown in this photograph), were reduced to rubble.

Standards of dress and general behaviour became more relaxed and uninhibited in the aftermath of the Great War. In this fashion photograph the mannequin is posing in a short, flowing diaphanous dress that reveals an amount of bare flesh that would have been scandalous a decade earlier.

One Sunday in April near Reigate Hill in Surrey. The motor car gave more and more people mobility and freedom of the roads at weekends. By the end of the previous year British motor-vehicle registrations had topped the million mark, which reflected the trend in America and Europe.

A specially converted Rolls Royce car, with caterpillar-tracked rear wheels and front-wheel skis, used by the revolutionary leader Vladimir Lenin (1870-1924) to commute to and from the Kremlin in Moscow while he was head of the Soviet government.

A rare photograph of Adolf Hitler (1889-1945) in 1924 after his release from imprisonment for trying to overthrow the Bavarian government in a *putsch* at Munich. While in gaol he had written *Mein Kampf*, his declaration of political intent. Mussolini was already in power in Italy and Hitler was keen to take advantage of the economic crisis in Germany.

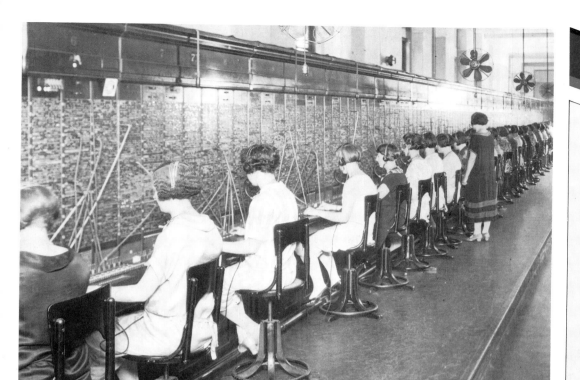

New York's vast new telephone exchange, opened in 1925, showing the new machinery. The increasing role played by women in business was seen by many as a step towards equality: but others recognised that the positions were lowly and regarded the movement as a new form of servitude.

The body assembly line at the Morris Motors works at Cowley. By 1925 Morris Motors employed 14,000 workers and produced a thousand cars a week.

1926

Sir Alan Cobham (1894-1973), one of the great early survey pilots, photographed in 1926, the year in which he made the first flight from Britain to Australia and back. On the return stage of the flight his co-pilot, A.B. Elliott, was killed by a stray Bedouin bullet. Cobham, whose exploits captured the public imagination, was knighted on his return and went on to pioneer commercial in-air flight refuelling.

Volunteers unloading milk churns at a food depot established in London's Hyde Park during the General Strike of 1926. The Strike, the climax to several years of industrial unrest, was called off after only nine days, partly because the government found no shortage of mainly middle-class volunteers — note the bowler hats — to keep essential services operating.

Greta Garbo (b.1905) co-starred with John Gilbert in *Flesh and the Devil* made in 1926 and released in 1927, the year in which the first 'talking film' *The Jazz Singer* also appeared. *Flesh and the Devil* was made shortly after Will Hayes had taken up his post in America to control the overt and increasing eroticism to be found in film. Garbo's beauty was legendary and her voice exciting; she went on to still greater success in a series of sound films. Gilbert was at this time a romantic idol to rival Valentino (who died in this year), but his career did not survive the coming of sound.

Dancing the Charleston, an uninhibited dance to jazz music that had its origins in American-negro music. Popular in Europe and America in the 1920s, the Charleston symbolised and expressed the new, looser sexual mores of the post-war generation.

Jack Dempsey (1895-1983), the 'Manassa Mauler', world champion heavyweight boxer, with the challenger, Gene Tunney (left), photographed before their famous title fight in Philadelphia on 23 September. Tunney won on points.

1927

A woman soldier in Chiang Kai-shek's nationalist army. In 1927 China was once again in chaos, ruled over by a number of petty warlords. Canton was controlled by the Kuomintang (republican nationals) who with Russian support, sent out an expedition under Chiang Kai-shek (1887-1975) to bring China under nationalist control.

American aviator Charles Lindbergh (1902-74) beside the airplane 'Spirit of St. Louis' in which in May he became a world hero as the first man to fly the Atlantic solo, taking 33½ hours. Five years later triumph turned to tragedy when his 2-year-old son was kidnapped and murdered.

Here in Shanghai, barbed wire defences go up around one of the European enclaves to protect it from the 'Bolshevist led' threatened Kuomintang attack.

1928 — 1938: Depression and Uncertainty. By the late 1920s the optimism born at the end of the Great War — as it was known by the victors — was waning. In America, the rise of Hollywood (p55) and the introduction, in 1927, of the 'talkies', the crusading age of journalism, the continued building of skyscrapers and other outward signs of expansion and prosperity were balanced by the continuing moral cost of Prohibition (p59 & p69).

Optimism finally cracked when, in 1929, panic selling on the New York stock exchange heralded the infamous Wall Street Crash (p58) and the start of the Depression, a world-wide slump in the international money market that led to massive unemployment and poverty (p60 & p66). At the same time, political uncertainty and mounting bitterness in Germany at the huge reparations demanded, in 1919, by the victors at the Treaty of Versailles paved the way for Hitler's rise to power (p52 & p68). The shape of the fourth decade of the 20th century was being mapped out: recession; political chaos in the Far East; the rise of fascism; and the Spanish Civil War (1936 — 1939), which many saw as a rehearsal for the conflict to come (p72 & p76).

Yet the same period brought the coming of the affordable motor car, the drive-in movie, the age of air travel, the great Hollywood musicals (p70) and Jesse Owens' success in the Berlin Olympics (p74). All of these were recorded by the camera, reported on film and featured in the newspaper, and so *seen* by millions. And another form of photography was about to start adding to the world's store of images: television had been invented in 1926, and by 1936 the BBC was running the world's first regular transmission service.

The established philosophical foundation of science was subtly undermined by German-born physicist Albert Einstein (1879 — 1955) who, aged 26, published his special theory of relativity in 1905, the year in which he investigated the nature of light and worked on visible proof of the molecular constitution of matter. In 1916 he published his general theory of relativity and in 1921 he won the Nobel prize for Physics for 'his work in the domain of theoretical physics'. By 1928 he was a household name throughout the western world and had yet to come into conflict, as a pacifist and a Jew, with the Nazis. In 1932 he left Germany, he then resigned his positions in Berlin. He emigrated to the United States in 1933, and became an American citizen in 1940. Einstein stated that *E*nergy and *m*ass are equivalent, if *m* units of mass can be made to disappear mc^2 units of energy are liberated, *c* being the speed of light.

1929

An interested but unconcerned crowd throngs outside the doors of the New York stock exchange in 1929. Inside panic selling on the stock market (13 million shares changed hands in a single day) led to the Wall Street Crash, to failures of banks and businesses, to rapidly rising unemployment and to a world-wide Depression.

The showcard tells the story as one investor who has lost all his money puts up his car for sale in the aftermath of the Wall Street Crash. Times were to become tougher still and hundreds of thousands of Americans were soon to be reduced to far greater hardships than the need to sell cheaply an expensive car.

$100 WILL BUY THIS CAR MUST HAVE CASH LOST ALL ON THE STOCK MARKET

The German airship *Graf Zeppelin*, which is seen here in Los Angeles after crossing the Pacific from Tokyo, made the first airship flight around the world in August.

Prohibition legalised boot-legging and then wider offences in the minds of many. For a while — until the cost became apparent — this led to a wide spread public fascination with the world of crime. Here the bullet-ridden bodies of five mobsters lined up and gunned down by members of Al Capone's gang lie where they fell in what became known as the Saint Valentine's Day Massacre, Chicago.

1930

Britain suffered like the rest of the world in the Depression that followed the Wall Street Crash. By July there were two million unemployed in Britain and by the end of the year two and a half million. Here police try unsuccessfully to restrain unemployed demonstrators on London's Tower Hill in March.

The wreckage of the British airship R101, which flew into a hill forty miles from Paris at Beauvais in France on 5 October while on its way to India. The tragedy put a stop to the development of commercial passenger airships in Britain.

In Chicago the gangster Al Capone (1895-1947) opened in 1930 a soup kitchen to feed the city's homeless and unemployed, partly for publicity, but also partly perhaps in gratitude for escaping conviction for his crimes earlier in the year when he was freed for lack of evidence against him.

Throughout the 1930s the Handley Page 42 Hannibal four-engined airliner was the backbone of the Imperial Airway's fleet. The Hannibal first flew on 14 November 1930 and in June 1931 went into regular passenger service (on the London-Paris route), bringing higher standards of comfort and reliability to air travel.

British aviator Amy Johnson (1903-41) in the de Havilland Gipsy Moth *Jason* in which she became the first woman to fly solo from England to Australia, in 19½ days, in May.

The Indian nationalist leader Mahatma Gandhi (1869-1948), campaigner for Indian independence from the British Empire, leads his supporters on a 100-mile march from Ahmedabad to the Gulf of Cambay, during which the marchers distilled salt from sea water to protest against the government's salt monopoly. He was jailed but quickly released and summoned to London for talks.

King Alfonso XIII of Spain, shown here in army uniform in the early 1920s when his troops were fighting Arab nationalists in Morocco, fled his kingdom on 14 April after he had failed in his attempt to set up a dictatorship and the republicans had been trumphant in the 1931 municipal elections. In 1975 his grandson became one of the few members of a royal family ever to make a successful return to popular monarchy.

The Supermarine S.6B, outright winner of the Schneider Trophy, 29 September. On the same day another S.6B set up a new world air speed record of 407.02 m.p.h., becoming the first aircraft ever to exceed a speed of 400 m.p.h. The British classic World War II fighter plane, the Supermarine Spitfire, was developed from this racing seaplane.

Mahatma Gandhi leaving 10 Downing Steet, London, 4 December, after a meeting with the British prime minister Ramsay MacDonald. Gandhi had been released from prison to come to London to attend a round-table conference on the future of India.

The Swiss physicist Auguste Piccard (1884-1962) photographed in the gondola of the balloon with which he had just reached a world record altitude of just under 10 miles. His feat was possible because the gondola carried its own supply of air, a technique that was followed by all later high-altitude balloonists.

The opening ceremony, 19 March, of the Sydney Harbour Bridge. This was the world's longest steel arch bridge and it carried the world's widest bridge carriageway — two rail tracks, eight road lanes, a footpath and cycle tracks.

'Bonus City', Washington, where army veterans set up their camp in June and demanded to be paid compensation owed for their war service. Thousands of penniless, homeless, unemployed veterans poured into the camp to form the 'Bonus Army' during the early years of the Depression.

One feature of the Depression in America was a craze for dance marathons — in which poverty-stricken couples danced until they dropped with exhaustion and only the thought of the prize money kept the survivors going. This one, in New York in 1932, offered the winning couple the money to pay for their marriage licence.

Sir Malcolm Campbell (1885-1949) with his schoolboy son Donald (at the wheel of the Campbell Special, *Bluebird*), 9 January, before leaving for Daytona Sands, Florida, where he was to better his own land speed record with a speed of 272.46 m.p.h.

In what was then the world's worst air disaster the United States navy dirigible *Akron* crashed into the sea during a violent storm, 4 April. All 73 people on board were killed, including Rear Admiral Moffett, head of the Navy Bureau of Aeronautics. Just as the crash of the *R101* had killed public confidence in airships in Britain; so the crash of the *Akron* destroyed the American public's belief in the future of airship travel.

Adolf Hitler driving through Berlin with German President Paul von Hindenburg, who had appointed him Chancellor, in January. Four weeks later Hitler used the Reichstag Fire as an excuse for rushing through the 'Enabling' Act that made him dictator of Germany, and deprived parliament of control of the budget, foreign policy and legislation.

In the skies over the Himalayas: one of the two Westland Wallace biplanes that made the first flights over the summit of Mount Everest, 3 April, flying over the peaks between Nepal and Tibet.

In the United States the gangsters were still a public danger in 1933. Three detectives and an armoured car were thought necessary to bring mobster Frank Zimmermann from Washington to Chicago for his trial. The car is armoured in steel plate, has bullet-proof glass and is fitted with gun-ports through which the tommy guns carried by the police could be fired.

1934

Fred Astaire (b.1899), whom Rudolf Nureyev once described as 'the world's greatest dancer' — with the most magical of film dance partners, Ginger Rogers (b.1911) in a scene from *The Gay Divorcée* (1934), one of a series of superb, bright musicals they made together between 1933 and 1939, during the latter days of the Depression.

Civil war in Austria. Chancellor Dollfuss (1892-1934) suspended parliamentary government in 1933. The following February socialist workers in Vienna demonstrated and Dollfuss called out the army, ordering an assault on workers' housing estates in the Vienna suburbs. The socialists were quickly defeated after machine-gun detachments like this one opened fire on the tenements.

Joseph Goebbels (1897-1945), Hitler's Minister for Propaganda and National Enlightenment, reviewing a Nazi guard of honour before addressing a meeting in Danzig, 8 April. At this time Danzig was a Free City administered by the League of Nations, but it had an elected Senate which was dominated by the Nazis. Four years after this, Hitler's demands that Danzig — later *Gdansk* — be annexed to Germany were a factor in the start of World War II.

Italian soldiers, on leave from Abyssinia, march through the streets of Rome. One of them, with full beard, looks as though he has just arrived from the front. Mussolini's troops invaded Abyssinia on 2 October. The League of Nations condemned the aggression and imposed sanctions, but failed to deter Mussolini.

1936

Refugees from a Spain wracked by civil war seek sanctuary over the French border. The Spanish Civil War (1936-9) was an ideological foretaste and, for the fascists at least, a practical rehearsal of World War II.

Flames over Madrid, 2 December, after a night air raid. Madrid was held by republican government forces and besieged by the insurgent nationalists of General Francisco Franco (1892-1975), whose planes mounted a series of air raids.

Opposite: 'After I am gone', George V stated, 'the boy will ruin himself in twelve months'. Edward VIII inspects HMS *Royal Oak*, November. He abdicated the following month, his passion for divorcée Wallis Simpson having precipitated a bitter, brief constitutional crisis. In the event, the man groomed for monarchy reigned for slightly less than a year.

Black American athlete Jesse Owens (1913-80) winning the 200 metres, in record time, at the 1936 Berlin Olympics. Owens' spectacular and much publicised successes at the Games, which Hitler had intended to be a showplace for Aryan supremacy, made a public mockery of Nazi ideas on race.

In Britain, unemployment caused by the decline of the traditional manufacturing industries and by the Depression was regional in its impact; to a large extent the north-east suffered while the south-east prospered. In the Durham town of Jarrow two thirds of the adult male population were out of work and they set out on a march to London — here photographed passing through a quiet Buckinghamshire village on 26 October — to demand government action. World War II was to revitalise industry.

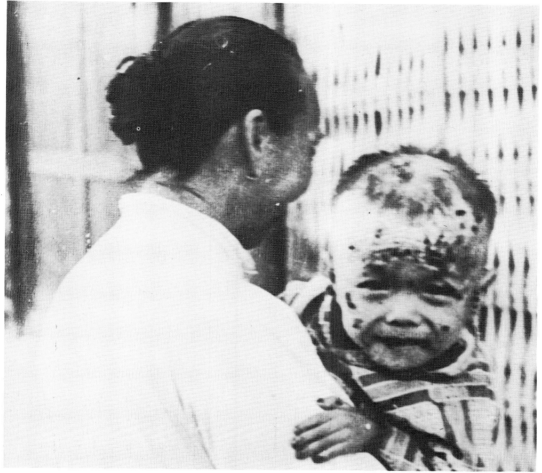

A Chinese mother carries her injured child to the safety of the International Settlement during a bombardment of Shanghai, 21 September, in the Sino-Japanese War. Japanese forces occupied the city a few weeks later.

In this rare 1937 photograph an American journalist sits between the two men who were to become the leaders of modern China. Left is Mao Tse-Tung (1893-1976), who was to become first Chairman of the People's Republic of China in 1949; right is Chu Teh (1886-1976), creator and commander-in-chief of the Chinese Red Army. Both men had been leaders of the epic 8,000-mile Long March which took place between October 1934 and October 1935, but both by 1937 were turning their energies to the defeat of the Japanese invaders.

In the second year of the Spanish Civil War the tide began to turn in favour of Franco's nationalist insurgent forces. Here, in a public square in Oviedo in northern Spain, nationalists proudly display a crudely-made armoured car captured from government troops.

Eight hundred foot long and weighing 242 tons, the world's largest airship, the German *Hindenburg*, becomes a flaming pyre at its mooring mast at Lakehurst, New Jersey. In this, the last major airship disaster, thirty-five people were killed. Fire engulfed the airship within seconds because it was hydrogen-filled; the United States having refused to supply Germany with inert helium gas. The age of the airship was over, leaving air travel clear for commercial airliners to become the main form of international transport.

The Duke of Windsor, the former King Edward VIII, and his duchess meet Adolf Hitler in 1938. At one time Hitler at least toyed with the idea of 'restoring' the duke to the British throne as a puppet king.

By the late 1930s the American and his car could hardly bear to be parted. The first drive-in cinema opened at Camden, New Jersey, in 1934 and many more followed. This is the Drive-In Theatre at Los Angeles, opened in 1938. 'Motorists', rejoiced the press handout, 'can now visit the cinema and watch the films without taking the trouble of parking or even getting out of their cars.' The car also revolutionised courtship habits; in three of the four cars closest to the camera in this photograph the occupants are using the back seats.

British prime minister Neville Chamberlain (1869-1940) arriving at Munich airport for peace talks with Hitler, Mussolini and Edouard Daladier (1884-1970), the French prime minister. On his return to England Chamberlain flourished for the cameras a scrap of paper which, he claimed, guaranteed 'peace in our time'.

German troops (still using horse-drawn transport) pass a frontier customs post and enter the Sudetenland region of Czechoslovakia, 2 October. Most of the population of the Sudetenland was German, and there had been a persistent and carefully orchestrated campaign for the integration of the Sudetenland into Germany. The British prime minister Neville Chamberlain had sanctioned Hitler's annexation of the Sudetenland at the Munich Agreement of 29 September.

Robert Capa's famous photograph of the terror and confusion of battle; a prisoner is brought in during the Spanish Civil War. Whether the prisoner is nationalist or republican, what his fate was to be and where the photograph was taken — none of these things is known for certain and none of these things matter. This is a photograph of man at war.

Shirley Temple (b1928) was at the peak of her box-office appeal in the second half of the 1930s. To the modern eye the photograph seems more embarrassing than appealing — an embarrassment compounded in this scene from *Rebecca of Sunnybrook Farm* (1938) by the appearance with her of an Uncle Tom character played by the great tap-dancer Bill Robinson (1878-1949).

The American actor and film director Orson Welles (1915-1985) earned early notoriety when, on Halloween Night 1938, he directed a radio broadcast of H. G. Wells' *The War of the Worlds* which was so realistic that it caused a widespread panic among its American audience, who were convinced that the earth really was being invaded by Martians. In Groves Mill, New Jersey the residents panicked and shot up a local water tower having mistaken it for a Martian.

1939

Polish cavalrymen make a massed charge on manoeuvres in April. Poland was attacked by Germany at dawn on 1 September and its army proved no match for the Germans. 'Their horse cavalry', wrote Winston Churchill, '. . . charged valiantly against the swarming tanks and armoured cars, but could not harm them with their swords and lances.'

1939 — 1962: War and Cold War. Photographs such as Robert Capa's picture of a prisoner being brought across the line (p79) and newsreel reports sent around the world from the Spanish Civil War and the war between Japan and China (p75), had ensured even before the second world war started that people had seen the face of modern conflict.

When combined with a strong memory of the Great War as an unnecessary, costly waste of a generation, this ensured that the Western democracies remained until the end of the 1930s as unwilling to enter a second world war as they had — in the main — been enthusiastic to enter the first.

In one of this century's major ironies, the war that did start in 1939 as an attempt by the Allies to prevent Poland being swallowed by the Nazi regime (p80) — and which America joined actively in 1942, following Pearl Harbor (p90) — ended in 1945 with not only Poland but almost all of Eastern Europe under the domination of Russia. Hitler's original ally in the 1939 partition of Poland.

This irony led the world's major powers straight from world war to cold war, the stalemate of superpower confrontation: in 1956 the Soviet invasion of Hungary (p120) and the disaster of Suez (p119) discredited for most of the West any remaining faith in either communism or the value of colonial power.

Just before this, the 'certainty' of the Red Menace/Yellow Peril days of post-war late 1940s and early 1950s — with their witch hunts fuelled by film, television and newspaper — began to collapse in 1954, aided by newsman Ed Murrow's televised attack on McCarthyism in America.

For the post-war world, the development of the atomic bomb, and its use by America in Japan in 1945, besides producing the cold war, transformed the basis of international power from its old established colonial and imperial base towards a new technological foundation, established primarily by America.

As 1939 opened in Spain the republican forces began to collapse before sweeping advances in Catalonia by nationalist troops under General Franco. Here, an Italian plane is being loaded with ammunition to take part in the assault that led, within ten days, to the fall of Barcelona.

A ski patrol of the Finnish army in action against invading Russian troops during the fiercely fought, but one-sided, fifteen-week war (30 November 1939 – 12 March 1940) that gave Russia vast areas of Finnish territory.

Madrid fell to nationalist forces led by General Francisco Franco on 28 March and all fighting in the Spanish Civil War ended three days later. The fascist salute offered by these citizens of Madrid as they welcome a victorious tank crew shows unambiguously the collapse of the city and the political flavour of the new regime.

Clark Gable (1901-60) and Vivien Leigh (1913-67) as Rhett Butler and Scarlett O'Hara in *Gone with the Wind* a 'masterpiece' of popular entertainment, (released in 1939), which must be one of the most famous films of all time. It was for many years the longest (220 minutes). It also put into currency the phrase 'Frankly my dear, I don't give a damn.'

As Britain stood on the threshold of World War II, at the beginning of 1939, it still had over one million unemployed. This demonstration, one of many, was held in Trafalgar Square, London. 'Ernie' Brown, whose attention is drawn to the skull, was the then Minister of Labour.

King Zog of Albania, Europe's only Muslim king, who lost his throne when his country was taken over by Italy in April. Mussolini wanted Albania for use as a stepping stone in an invasion of Greece.

This bizarre photograph of a scantily clad London chorus girl wearing her gas mask was used as part of the official campaign to take the terror out of wearing gas masks. One of the great British fears at the beginning of World War II was that the country would be attacked, from the air, with poison gas. Gas masks — 38 million of them — were distributed to all civilians, men, women, children and babies. Government propaganda stressed the importance of becoming familiar with their use.

Russian casualties, frozen stiff in the attitudes in which they died, awaiting burial after Finnish troops had over-run their positions in northern Finland. This small Finnish success was against the general run of the war, soon to end in Russian victory.

Churchill stands here, 5 August, with a tommy gun, a jutting cigar and a Churchillian hat in a pose that epitomises the aggressive determination he brought to his war leadership. Winston Churchill became British prime minister on 10 May, on the very day that German armies invaded the Netherlands, Belgium and Luxembourg.

A queue of British soldiers wades to one of the rescue ships that evacuated nearly 340,000 British and French troops from Dunkirk in May, after the British Expeditionary force had been cut off by the lightning German armoured advance through France. Dunkirk was hailed as a miracle in a relieved Britain; more soberly, Winston Churchill pointed out that, 'Wars are not won by evacuations.'

Opposite: Children of hop pickers in the Kentish countryside take cover in a trench and watch a dog-fight over their heads as the German and British air forces fight the Battle of Britain in the skies above southern England in the summer and autumn of 1940.

Russian-born aircraft designer Igor Sikorsky (1889-1972) flies the VS-300, which made its first free flight, in the United States, on 13 May. The Germans had already flown a successful twin-rotor helicopter four years before but the VS-300 became the world's first practical and reliable single-rotor helicopter.

An occupying soldier talking with a British policeman on Jersey, one of the Channel Islands over run by the Germans in July. The police continued to function under German rule while the law courts continued to act in the King's name, though under German orders.

Hitler smiles benignly down upon his 'youngest S.A. man.'

Opposite: Adolf Hitler enters Paris and parades beneath the Eiffel Tower after the fall of France in June. There had been no battle for Paris — the city was evacuated on 13 June to save it from destruction.

1941

London's pigeons and London's sense of humour both survived the blitz. This photograph was taken in May, when the capital's ordeal by bombing was almost over; although the V1s and V2s were still to come.

The 'Desert Fox', Erwin Rommel (1891-1944), Commander of the German Afrika Korps, watches the test-firing of a 75mm gun, captured by the British from the Italians but then recaptured by the Germans. The gun's changes of ownership typify the to and fro of the war in north Africa during 1941. The Allies began the year with victories over the Italians but, with the arrival of Rommel, were soon driven into a retreat that was not reversed until the arrival of Montgomery.

The classic photograph that symbolised the spirit and sense of unity of the British people (summed up in the slogan 'Britain Can Take It') as they endured the blitz — the dome of St Paul's cathedral looms undamaged through the smoke from the burning buildings of the city of London.

Shelterers settle down for the night while some passengers still wait for late trains, January. London was bombed nightly from 7 September to 2 November 1940 and more intermittently thereafter. Londoners learned to cope with the danger and the destruction; an estimated one in seven of them spent every night in the deep underground stations, despite official objections. In the end officialdom had to yield to demand and even, after a time, to provide shelter equipment.

The Japanese surprise attack on the American naval base at Pearl Harbor, 7 December, inflicted in less than an hour greater naval losses than the United States had sustained throughout World War I. In the two and a half months following Pearl Harbor, the Japanese successfully invaded Malaya and the Philippines and captured Hong Kong, Manila and Singapore, but by bringing the United States into the war, Japan ensured her eventual defeat together with that of the other Axis powers.

Australia considered itself in real danger of invasion by the Japanese in 1942, with Japanese aircraft raiding Darwin and other Australian towns; and on 31 May Japanese submarines almost managed to enter Sydney Harbour. Here a coastal artillery battery of the United States army, stationed 'somewhere in Australia', fires its heavy gun.

By the autumn of 1942 the Germans had reached the farthest extent of their penetration of Russian territory; from then on they were to be driven inexorably back. In Britain support for Russia showed itself in gestures of friendship (Mrs Churchill raised a fund for Russia) and, more politically, in demands for a Second Front to relieve the pressure on 'our beleaguered Ally'. Photographs like this, showing a Red Army soldier in the field with an anti-tank rifle watching alertly for signs of the enemy, appeared regularly in British newspapers.

Italian soldiers captured in the second Battle of El Alamein, 23 October-4 November. The battle, fought by the British 8th Army under the command of General Bernard Montgomery (1887-1976), turned the tide of war in North Africa. His army covered 1400 miles in 18 weeks. Within six months all Axis resistance had ended in North Africa.

Face to face — the German general von Thoma, captured by a British tank squadron during the Battle of El Alamein, offers a salute to his enemy commander, General Montgomery. The two generals dined together at Montgomery's desert headquarters that evening and exchanged courtesies; von Thoma inviting Montgomery to visit him in Germany after the war.

In May when Winston Churchill went to Washington to settle with President Franklin Roosevelt their strategy for the Allied invasion of Europe, he gave his by then famous V-sign for the benefit of British sailors on the ship that had carried him across the Atlantic.

From July 1942 onwards the Nazis deported from the Warsaw ghetto many thousands of Jews to extermination camps. At last, in April 1943, the Jews of the ghetto fought back, with home-made grenades and incendiaries and weapons smuggled in through the sewers. They held out for weeks and were overcome only when tanks were brought in against them. The survivors (shown here) were taken from the burning ruins of the ghetto to the concentration camps.

1944

The battle for Cassino was one of the bloodiest in the Allied invasion of Italy. The monastery on top of its war-scarred mount was bombed on 15 February but it was not until 18 May that British and Polish troops took Monte Cassino and opened the way to Rome.

Young fighter pilots of the United States Army Air Force based in Britain are briefed by their commanding officer before a mission.

Opposite: One of the war's most evocative photographs. A woman air-raid warden comforts a terrified girl lifted from the ruins of her home after a German air attack on London in June 1944. The destruction may have been caused by a V1 flying-bomb; the first of these new weapons had fallen in Kent ten days before.

Perhaps the last photograph of Adolf Hitler, taken on his 56th birthday, 20 April. Haggard and exhausted, he inspects child soldiers who remained with him to defend Berlin against a Russian army already at the outskirts. Ten days later Hitler took his own life in the bunker beneath the ruins of his Chancellery.

With the defeat of Japan the Chinese nationalist leader Chiang Kai-shek and communist leader Mao Tse-tung met at Chiang's capital, Chungking, in the hope of agreeing some form of cooperation for post-war China. The talks came to nothing and civil war broke out again. The Americans withdrew their forces from China in 1947 and cut their aid to the Kuomintang: Mao eventually won in 1949.

In the Far East the Japanese were driven back from their conquests by a successful American offensive. United States marines raise the Stars and Stripes on the Pacific Island of Iwo Jima on 17 March, after three weeks of hellish battle. Iwo Jima was to have been a stepping stone for the invasion of the Japanese mainland.

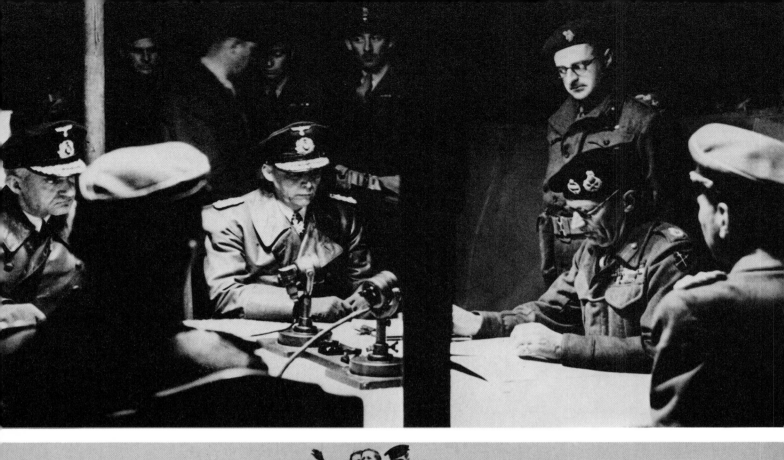

Previous page: Field Marshal Montgomery receives the surrender of the German forces in northwest Germany, the Netherlands and Denmark, 4 May.

Previous page: London celebrates victory: revellers in Parliament Square on VE Day, 8 May, which prime minister Winston Churchill officially proclaimed as the day of celebration of the end of the war in Europe.

The mushroom cloud of an atomic explosion rises above the Japanese city of Nagasaki, 9 August 1945. The mushroom cloud was to become the twentieth century's strongest and most frightening image.

'From now onward,' wrote Arthur Koestler, 'mankind will have to live with the idea of its death as a species.' The world's first atomic bomb was dropped on the Japanese city of Hiroshima on 6 August 1945. Following the bombing of Nagasaki, Japan surrendered rather than risk a similar attack on Tokyo.

1946

The victorious Allies set up a War Crimes Court at Nuremberg to try as war criminals a number of Nazi leaders. On the left, in the front row of the dock, is Hermann Goering (1893-1946), Hitler's Reichsmarshal, who was condemned to death by the court but avoided execution by committing suicide. Next to him is Rudolf Hess (b 1894), the former deputy leader of the Nazi party, who five years before had flown to Scotland to try and negotiate peace with the British government. Eleven of the leaders were convicted by the Allies and hanged, and seven — including Hess — were sentenced to terms of imprisonment.

Thousands of British women married American G.I.s who had been stationed in Britain during World War II. When the war ended, government money paid for the women's emigration to America. Here 'G.I. Brides' embark on the specially chartered liner *Argentina* for their journey to their new lives.

Earl Mountbatten of Burma (1900-1979) was appointed Viceroy of India in February. Within five months he had handed power over to two new dominions, Hindu India and Muslim Pakistan. Here, on the eve of independence, he sits with Jawaharlal Nehru (1889-1964), who was to be India's first prime minister, in the viceregal palace at New Delhi.

An illegal immigrant ship, crammed with nearly 2,700 Jewish refugees after British Naval interception off Palestine, April. The British clung to their hope that the British mandated territory might become a bi-national Jewish-Arab state; and tried to hold a population balance by limiting Jewish immigration into Palestine in the aftermath of World War II. Failure was recognised in November, when the United Nations decided to partition the country into Jewish and Arab states.

This could be a galaxy of Hollywood stars posing for a publicity photocall, but in fact it is a deputation, led by the fine actor and rare personality Humphrey Bogart (1899-1957) (second left, back row), arriving in Washington in October to protest at the way in which some of their colleagues were being branded as communists by the senate committee investigating 'un-American' activities.

As European borders were redrawn by the Allies after World War II, new refugees were added to those millions already made homeless and exiled by the war itself. These children had been driven from their homes in East Prussia and have arrived at Meissen, in Soviet-occupied Germany, where they wait, with their belongings, for the Russians to find them new homes.

THE IMPORTANT THING IN THE OLYMPIC GAMES IS NOT WINNING BUT TAKING PART. THE ESSENTIAL THING IN LIFE IS NOT CONQUERING BUT FIGHTING WELL.

BARON de COUBERTIN

The Olympic Games that should have been held in Tokyo in 1940 and in London in 1944 had been cancelled because of war, so when the revived Games opened in London in 1948 they were as much a celebration of peace as a celebration of sport. Over 80,000 spectators — among them King George VI (1894-1952) — watched the torch-bearer carry the Olympic flame into the Wembley arena.

The paper that got it wrong —
president-elect Harry S. Truman
(1884-1972) grins as he holds up
for the cameras an early edition
newspaper that assumed, on the
strength of the first election
returns, Truman's defeat in the
1948 presidential elections.
Truman had succeeded to the
presidency on Franklin
Roosevelt's death in office in 1945
and had taken the decision to
drop atomic bombs on Japan. His
re-election for a second term
surprised not only the *Chicago
Daily Tribune* but most
commentators as well.

At Haifa — in front of interested
photographers — the Union
Jack is lowered for the last time
as the last remaining British
troops and administrators leave
Palestine. The British mandate
ended at midnight on 14 May;
and Palestine was without a
British military presence for the
first time since 1917.

Breaking the Berlin blockade —
an American C-74 Globemaster
transport plane is unloaded at
Gatow airport, in the British
sector, during the Berlin airlift.
Berlin had fallen to the Red
Army, but America, Britain and
France were given zones of
occupation in the city and had
access to it along 'corridors'
from West Germany. In the
summer of 1948 the Russians
halted all road and rail traffic
coming from the west, thus
blockading Berlin. The
Americans and British
successfully supplied the city by
air until after the Russians
ended the blockade in May
1949.

Sweets came off ration in Britain in 1949, as did clothes and textiles. Bread and potatoes were already de-rationed, all part of the post-war Labour government's desire, as the next general election drew near, to lift controls and get the British economy moving. Here, in a London street market, sweets are freely on sale for the first time in nearly seven years.

The summary street execution of two communist 'criminals' in Shanghai, early 1949. The Kuomintang executioner may well shortly have fallen victim to a similar fate — the victorious communist forces drove out the nationalists, occupied Shanghai in May, and began their own series of executions.

The body of an Iron Age man was found mummified in a peat bog at Tollund in Denmark in 1950, after being buried for at least two thousand years. The man, who had been strangled with a leather thong, was probably a sacrificial victim. The discovery refired interest in pre-Christian behaviour and customs.

British troops in Korea, 1950. British units were sent by Britain's Labour government to form part of the United Nations force; Britain also gave substantial naval aid. The British troops were badly equipped and were forced to borrow American clothing to survive the winters.

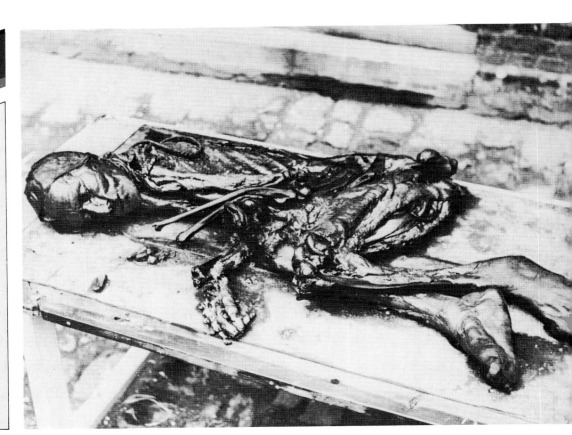

General Douglas MacArthur (1880-1964) was appointed commander of the United Nations forces in South Korea in June, after North Korea had invaded the South across the 38th parallel and the Security Council had called upon UN member states to help repel the invasion. On 15 September he landed a force of marines at Inchon, 200 miles behind the enemy lines; here, leading as always from near the front, he comes ashore with his men. MacArthur was driven back in 1951 when China joined the North, and he was replaced by General Ridgeway who re-occupied the South; an armistice was signed in 1953.

The French couturier Christian Dior (1905-1957) — who had introduced to Europe the first big new post-war fashion, the 'New Look' — gave his first London show, at the Savoy Hotel, on 25 April. Here he presents seven of his evening dresses.

1951

Photographs, like this one, of giant humanoid footprints in the snow made the Yeti, or Abominable Snowman, into an international household name in 1951, when a British mountaineering expedition brought the photographs back from the Himalayas. Rumours of the existence of the Yeti had come out of Nepal a hundred years before, but there had been no reliable sightings. Yeti-hunts organised on the strength of the 1951 photographs failed to sight — much less capture — any of the mythical half-human, half-bear creatures.

In Korea a battery of 155mm self-propelled guns of the United Nations forces puts down a barrage on enemy-held positions north of the 38th parallel, April. China had by now entered the war in support of the North Koreans.

Troops of the American 11th Airborne Division watch — 'at a safe distance' — the detonation of an atomic bomb at Frenchman's Flat, in the Nevada desert. The bomb, dropped from a B29 bomber, was exploded less than a thousand feet above the ground. The paratroopers were the first soldiers in history to participate in 'atomic war games'.

Joe Louis (1914-1981), the 'Brown Bomber' and world heavyweight boxing champion, had retired in 1949 but he had a comeback fight, on 28 October at Madison Square Garden with Rocky Marciano (1923-1969). Marciano scored a technical knock out by sending Joe Louis through the ropes in the eighth round.

1952

Britain's new queen, Elizabeth II (b 1926), steps from the aircraft that has brought her from Kenya, where she had been staying when her father, George VI, died on 6 February 1952. Among the privy councillors meeting her are prime minister Winston Churchill, leader of the opposition Clement Attlee (1883-1967) and foreign secretary Anthony Eden (1897-1977).

A scientist examines a coelacanth. Until one was caught in the Indian Ocean in 1938, the coelacanth had been known only as a fossil in rocks 400 million years old. The 1938 specimen had been identified from a sketch; only in 1952 were three more caught and, this time, preserved for laboratory examination. To find the coelacanth still living was, one scientist exclaimed, 'like seeing a dinosaur walking down the street!'

Disaster at the Farnborough air show, 6 September. The prototype de Havilland 110 twin-engined fighter plane disintegrated in the air, killing its crew of two as well as 28 spectators on the ground.

Opposite: Kikuyu women, in an attempt to free 500 Kikuyu men held in detention, march on a police station in Kenya, where the refusal of white settlers to give representation to the black majority led, in October, to acts of violence instigated by the Mau Mau — a nationalist secret society of the Kikuyu tribe. Mau Mau's leader, Jomo Kenyatta (1897-1978), was imprisoned by the colonial government but later became President of Kenya.

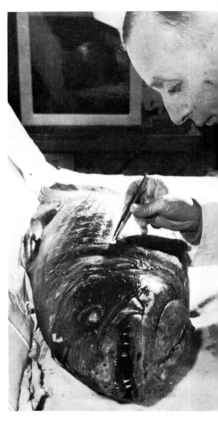

French paratroopers landing near the Vietminh-held town of Langson in Indo-China. The French held on more grimly to the remnants of their Far Eastern empire than did the British. The French fought the Vietminh resistance movement — later renamed Vietcong — from 1946 until 1954, when Vietminh leader Ho Chi-Minh launched an attack and captured Dien Bien Phu after a 55-day siege and a final battle lasting 20 hours.

The bathyscaphe *Trieste*, a deep-sea research vessel sponsored by the United States navy, in which Auguste Piccard and his son descended to a depth of 1.967 miles/3.168 metres. The sea, mountain tops, Antarctica and soon the reaches of space were targets for ambitious exploration in the 1950s.

Opposite: The impressive family group photograph taken at Buckingham Palace after the coronation of Elizabeth II on 2 June. There was much talk at the time of a new forward-looking Elizabethan age; the pageantry of the coronation was, however, backward-looking — even though, for the first time in history, the ceremony was televised and millions around the world watched as a young woman was ritually changed into a queen.

Opposite: New Zealand mountaineer Edmund Hillary (b 1919) and Sherpa Tensing Norgay (1914-1986) of the British Everest Expedition — which was led on the lines of a military exercise by Colonel John Hunt (b 1910) — reached the 29,028-feet-high (8,854 metres) summit of the world's highest mountain on 29 May. The news — together with this photograph — arrived in Britain neatly on the morning of the coronation; and in America announcers broke into programmes on radio and television to relay the news.

1954

The British 25-year-old middle-distance runner Roger Bannister (b 1929) about to become the first man in the world to run the mile in under four minutes. A medical student, Bannister broke through the four-minute mile barrier at Oxford, on 6 May with a time of 3 minutes 59.4 seconds.

Art met the media when the Spanish painter Salvador Dali, best known and most exhibitionist of the surrealists, showed off 'Soft Self Portrait' to a 1954 press conference which he called to announce his renunciation of surrealism and his 'rebirth' as a cubist.

SOFT SELF PORTRAIT

The Mau Mau revolt was determinedly opposed by the colonial and British forces in Kenya. On 24 April, in one operation, five thousand troops and police moved in on Nairobi and rounded up thousands of Kikuyu and other tribesmen. Suspects detained in the raid are here lined up, ready to be carried off to detention camps.

1955

'Say No to the Statute' advises the poster in the Saar district of Germany. In a bitterly-fought plebiscite held on 23 October the Saarlanders followed the poster's advice, voting against the 'Europeanisation' of the French-occupied Saar and for its integration with Germany. The coal-rich Saar finally became West Germany's tenth state over a year later on 2 January 1957.

The young American actor James Dean (1931-1955) became a symbol both of and for rebellious youth after starring in the film *Rebel Without a Cause* (1955). A speed addict and a devotee of fast cars (he holds here two of his road-racing trophies), he was killed in a car crash in 1955 and posthumously promoted to the status of a cult hero. The idea of 'youth' as a potent commercial force was just beginning to be accepted — and the young's custom courted — by entrepreneurs in the West.

The aftermath of the worst accident in the history of motor racing; in the 1955 Le Mans 24-hour Race a Mercedes-Benz driven by Pierre Levegh bounced over a safety barrier and plunged into a crowded public enclosure. Levegh and 83 spectators were killed.

An engagement portrait of Prince Rainier III of Monaco (b 1923) and his fiancée, American film actress Grace Kelly (1928-1982). The marriage, on 19 April, of the ruler of a tiny Mediterranean principality to a famous Hollywood star and 'ice-maiden' beauty (she had starred in three Hitchcock films) was an event the world's press found irresistible — to the sheltered prince's annoyance.

The crowd in Alexandria's Manchia Square, on 27 July, gathered to hear Egyptian president Gamal Nasser (1918-1970) announce the appropriation of the Suez Canal Company, whose shares were owned largely by the British government and French investors. Nasser proposed to use the revenues to finance the Aswan High Dam project on the Nile — from which America and Britain had just withdrawn a promise of financial aid. America and the UN declined to act, but Israel attacked in late October, followed by an Anglo/French offensive and the canal zone was re-occupied after four days' fighting.

Rioters in Budapest, Hungary, with the head of Joseph Stalin, part of a massive statue pulled down and wrecked — on 23 October — at the beginning of the Hungarian Rising. The rebels demanded greater 'democratisation', more national independence and higher living standards. Anti Soviet riots had already occurred in this year in Poland and, three years before, in East Berlin.

Soviet tanks put out of action by student and worker rebels of Budapest. The rebels demanded the withdrawal of Russian troops from Hungary, and Soviet forces did indeed begin to pull out of the country: but the reforms initiated by the new prime minster, Imre Nagy (1896-1958), were too much for the Soviet government to accept, and the Red Army moved back into Hungary and crushed the revolt.

American singer Bill Haley's international hit record *Rock Around the Clock* (1955) established him as a leading force in the pop world. When he arrived at Waterloo Station in London in February he was greeted by a phenomenon new to Britain — a mob of 'teenagers' who thrust the police aside in their rush to reach the singer.

A Japanese car on exhibition at the Paris motor show, October. Although outwardly similar to American and European cars, Japanese cars lagged behind in technical refinement, but were catching up fast with production rising from less than 50,000 in 1948 to over ¾ million in 1958.

The 250-foot steerable reflector bowl of the largest radio telescope in the world at Jodrell Bank in Cheshire. The telescope went into operation in October and almost immediately began tracking the world's first man-made satellite, Russia's *Sputnik I* which had been launched that month.

The American nuclear-powered submarine *Nautilus* arriving at Portland in Dorset after making the first crossing of the Arctic Ocean, underneath the ice. It had reached the North Pole, after 62 hours below the ice cap, on 3 August; its captain announced its achievement in a simple three-word radio message: 'Nautilus 90 North'.

Sir Vivian Fuchs (b 1908) (right), leader of the Commonwealth Transantarctic Expedition which crossed the Antarctic continent between 24 November 1957 and 2 March 1958, meets Sir Edmund Hillary at the South Pole. Fuchs' party had reached the Pole, roughly the halfway point of their journey, after trekking with sno-cats for 56 days; Hillary, whose New Zealand contingent had set up supply bases along the route, flew back to the Pole for the meeting.

Fidel Castro (b 1927) called for 'total war' against the Cuban dictator Fulgencio Batistá (1901-1973) in March and led an insurrection that, by the end of that year, was on the very edge of victory. These are guerilla fighters of Castro's army after they had captured, on 19 December, after a three-day siege, a government garrison town in central Cuba. Castro asked for and initially received American backing.

Soviet premier Nikita Krushchev (1894-1971) leaving a dinner given in his honour by the United Nations secretary-general Dag Hammarskjold (1905-1961) at the United Nations building in New York. Krushchev, who had become premier in the previous year, was a proponent of 'peaceful co-existence' and his visit to the United States was only one in a series of overseas visits he undertook in an attempt to lower world tension and restrain the cold war.

The 1959 Easter Aldermaston March sets out from the gates of the Atomic Weapons Research Establishment at Aldermaston on the first stage of its 53-mile protest march to Trafalgar Square in London. At the head of the column (extreme right) is Canon John Collins, the co-founder, with Bertrand Russell, of the Campaign for Nuclear Disarmament. The late 1950s were a time of growing popular support for the movement.

Previous page: An Avro Vulcan bomber of the Royal Air Force roars over the crowd at the Farnborough air show. It was thought by the Conservative government of the day that these bombers, which could carry and deliver hydrogen bombs, would be able to bear the main burden of Britain's independent nuclear deterrence while Blue Streak missiles were being developed.

This spectacular crash, at the 1959 German Grand Prix, had a happy ending. The driver, Hans Hermann, here crouched on the track as his disintegrating B.R.M. car somersaults over his head, escaped without injury.

The Dalai Lama of Tibet (seated, sixth from left) with the members of his personal guard who went with him to India when, like some 9,000 of his subjects, he fled from Tibet after a full scale but abortive revolt against Chinese occupation ended in Tibet becoming a completely subjugated province of China.

1960

American pop singer Elvis Presley (1935-1977) points to his new stripes after his promotion to sergeant in the United States Army. Presley, a major figure of Rock and Roll — and almost a symbol of America — was drafted into the army in 1958 and stationed for two years in Germany. Demobilised in 1960, he returned to his singing career, appearing in more than thirty popular but not critically acclaimed films. He died of an accidental drug overdose at the age of 42.

The victims of Sharpeville. On 21 March South African police opened fire on black demonstrators protesting against the laws that limited their movement and forced them to carry passes. Sixty-seven demonstrators were killed and nearly 200 wounded. The incident aroused a revulsion in the Commonwealth against apartheid that culminated in South Africa's decision to leave the Commonwealth in 1961.

The British colony of Nigeria gained its independence from Britain on 1 October. Its first independent prime minister, Tafawa Balewa (1912-1966) who had been colonial prime minister since 1957, is shown speaking at the formal independence ceremony in the presence of Princess Alexandra. Within a decade the country had passed through civil war into military rule.

Death comes to a Japanese politician, October. During a political rally in Tokyo a knife-wielding student, dodging officials who reached out to grab him, rushed at Inejiro Asanuma (right), chairman of Japan's socialist opposition party. Moments later Asanuma lay dying from stab wounds in the chest.

French armoured vehicles patrolling the outskirts of Algiers in December, during a savage guerilla war — fought with great cruelty on both sides — waged between the Algerian National Liberation Front and the French army. The Algerian war was ruinously costly to France; it had brought down the Fourth Republic in May 1958 and it was nearly to cost the life of president Charles de Gaulle (1890-1970), who had been recalled from retirement to deal with the crisis and who survived several assassination attempts organised by French army officers opposed to his determination to offer Algeria its independence.

In June the new American president, John F. Kennedy (1917-1963), met the Soviet premier Nikita Krushchev in Vienna. At this meeting Kennedy learned of the Russian intent to hand over the whole of Berlin, as a demilitarised city, to East Germany; and Krushchev then learned of America's determination to protect the independence of West Berlin.

Opposite: Building the Berlin Wall, thrown up overnight on 13 August to dam the stream of refugees from the East crossing into West Berlin, where all that a materialist society could offer was constantly on show: approximately 200,000 crossed in 1960 and 100,000 in the first half of 1961. The Wall quickly became a symbol of the mistrust and divide between East and West. 'Our world,' the great psychologist Carl Jung noted sadly, 'is dissociated like a neurotic, with the Iron Curtain marking the line of division'.

Opposite: The old Belgian Congo — now Zaire — was granted independence on 30 June, and promptly broke up in a series of complicated and savage civil wars and secessions. The copper-rich province of Katanga broke away and a separate regime also set itself up at Stanleyville (now Kisangani). In this photograph soldiers from this regime stand brutal guard over a group of young prisoners — probably mercenaries fighting on the side of Colonel Joseph Mobutu (b 1930) who as Chief of Staff announced that the army was taking supreme power.

Anthropologist Louis Leakey (1903-1972) with the skull of a man-like primate, an ancestor of *Homo sapiens*, that he unearthed from the Olduvai Gorge in Tanganyika (the skull on the left is that of a chimpanzee, there only to offer a comparison). Leakey's work was important for establishing East Africa as the likely place of origin of man.

Russian-born ballet dancer Rudolf Nureyev (b 1939) faces his first Western-style press conference in Paris, after defecting while on tour in France. His defection, although presented as a political coup by the West, was on artistic rather than political grounds; he claimed that the rigid structure of Soviet ballet cramped his creativity.

MISSILE ERECTOR

THEODOLITE STATION

5 TRUCKS UNDER
CAMOUFLAGE NETTING

MISSILE SHELTER TENTS

It was detailed aerial photographs like this that convinced United States president John F. Kennedy in October that Russia was introducing ballistic missiles with atomic warheads into Cuba. Kennedy promptly ordered a naval blockade of Cuba and called upon Russia to remove all missiles from the island; Kennedy also had troops ordered to Florida and over 150 missiles aligned on Russia. There followed a week of high tension — with the threat of nuclear war hanging over the world — before Russian premier Nikita Krushchev agreed to withdraw the weapons.

Until 1962 anyone holding a British passport could freely enter Britain, but from the late 1950s coloured immigrants came into the country in numbers large enough to be noticeable. On 1 July the Commonwealth Immigration Act restricted entry to immigrants who had a job to go to or who had special skills. These immigrants, landing at Southampton before the passing of the Act, were among the last to enter before the new rules came into force.

1963 — present: The Line of Division. 'Our world is dissociated like a neurotic, with the Iron Curtain marking the line of division.' So said the great psychologist Carl Jung about the Berlin Wall thrown up overnight in August 1961 to prevent people from East Berlin travelling to the West (p131). The cold war crisis reached its height during the Cuban missile crisis (p133) which for a week in 1962 had the world hanging on the brink of nuclear war.

An explosion of questioning popular culture, the invention of the contraceptive pill, a radical shift in the availability of consumer goods and the discovery by entrepreneurs that youth was a lucrative and easily identifiable market (p137 & p139) heralded the birth of the 'sixties': a decade which saw the asssassination of President Kennedy in 1963 (p136), the Soviet invasion of Czechoslovakia (p145) and the long and costly involvement of America, Australia and New Zealand in Vietnam, but which also saw the saving of the statues of Rameses II from Abu Simbel (p140), the first moon landing (p147), and the first heart transplant by Dr Christiaan Barnard (p142).

Equally important — if not more so in the long term — was the birth a decade later, in July 1978, of the world's first 'test tube' baby: while in 1986 the American shuttle disaster in January and the Soviet nuclear catastrophe at Chernobyl in April showed that if technology went wrong its price — both morally and politically — could be extremely high.

The world's first space woman, Valentina Tereshkova, who in June completed 48 orbits of the earth in the Russian spacecraft *Vostok 6*, only two years after the Russian test pilot Yuri Gagarin became the first person ever to travel in space. She later married a fellow cosmonaut and they had a daughter — the world's first child to be born of space travellers.

Opposite: One of the twentieth century's most powerful images: in an inferno of smoke and flame a Buddhist priest — suffering motionless and in silence — burns himself to death in a public square in Saigon in October. He was the fifth priest to kill himself in a series of ritual suicides protesting against continuing religious discrimination in South Vietnam. In this year the President of South Vietnam was assassinated in an American backed coup aimed at removing the then current Diem government.

President John F. Kennedy slumps in his seat and his wife, Jacqueline reaches out to him — in the moment after the United States president had been fatally shot by a rifleman from the fifth-floor window of a warehouse as he rode in a motorcade through the streets of Dallas, 22 November. The motive for the attack remains a mystery.

Lee Harvey Oswald (1939-1963), arrested and charged with the murder of John F. Kennedy, is himself shot and killed, by Dallas night-club owner Jack Ruby, as he is being taken from Dallas police station to the county gaol, 24 November.

The stark, geometric woman's hair style invented by London hairdresser Vidal Sassoon in 1964. Sassoon was one of a new band of creative designers and entrepreneurs — in every sphere from fashion, music and make-up to furniture and machinery — whose enterprise, innovative energy and flair for publicity gave the 1960s its popular cult status as a decade of freedom — for the West at least.

Ever since the former French colony of Laos had become independent in 1954 it had been wracked by a chronic and three-sided civil war, which was closely linked to the power struggles in neighbouring Vietnam and Cambodia. As always, it was the ordinary inhabitants who paid the price. Here villagers, fleeing from their homes before the advancing communist 'Pathet Lao' army, find temporary safety in a hastily constructed refugee camp.

Two American marines on a beach in Vietnam, December. Originally there had been only 4,000 advisors sent by President Kennedy, but direct and large-scale military involvement by the United States in the civil war in Vietnam began in 1965, after the communist Vietcong attacked American bases. Contingency plans had already been prepared by President L. B. Johnson to escalate the scale of the war. Bombing of North Vietnam began in February, United States marines landed in March, airborne troops in May and by August there were 125,000 American troops in Vietnam.

A fish-eye lens, looking vertically downwards, distorts the view from a balloon soaring above the Alps in the summer of 1965; and the mountain range is presented for the press as a psychedelic image.

It took boxer Cassius Clay less than sixty seconds to retain his hold on the world heavyweight championship on 25 May. He knocked out his opponent, Sonny Liston, in the first round. Here he taunts the floored challenger in front of the cameras, a sample of the way in which he mixed verbal and physical aggression throughout his career.

This 1966 Danish swimsuit was, according to the accompanying handout, one of 'the very first bathing suits in vinyl'. Man-made fabrics were much — and sometimes unsuitably — used in fashion in the mid-1960s. The chequered black-and-white pattern is an Op-Art design typical of its time, when appearance took on popular importance as a symbol of a new freedom given by the contraceptive pill and a booming economy.

A group of Red Guards — the young militants who spearheaded China's cultural revolution — reading a proclamation, by Mao Tse-tung's second-in-command Lin Piao, calling for a reassertion of Maoist principles. The cultural revolution which at first was widely acclaimed by intellectuals in America and Europe led to wholesale purges, torture and imprisonment of officials, writers and teachers — anyone thought to hold too-liberal attitudes.

Colossal statues of Ramesses II, from Abu Simbel, being reassembled, block by block, at a new site after being rescued from inundation by the rising waters penned up behind the Nile's new Aswan dam. Two 3,200-year-old temples, with their statues, were resited nearly 700 feet (213 metres) above their original position.

The four members of Britain's most successful pop group ever, the Beatles. From left, Paul McCartney (b 1942), George Harrison (b 1943), John Lennon (1940-1980) and Ringo Starr (b 1940) with − to the side − their astute manager, Brian Epstein, in a photograph taken after the members of the group had been awarded the M.B.E. in 1966. The award caused outrage in the British establishment, but no one could deny that pop was big business or that the financial rewards in terms of sales and exports were enormous.

England won the prestigious association football World Cup for the first − and so far only − time on 30 July. England met West Germany in the final and the match was a cliff-hanger − the winning goal being scored at the beginning of extra time and England's final goal in the last minute of extra time. A stamp was later issued to celebrate the event.

A soldier of the United States 101st airborne division in Vietnam carries his sign bearing its ironic and unlikely slogan.

Opposite: South African surgeon Christiaan Barnard (b 1922) photographed while performing an operation. In 1967 Barnard carried out the world's first heart transplant, replacing the heart of Louis Washkansky with that of a young girl killed a few hours earlier in a traffic accident. Washkansky survived the operation by only eighteen days, but the operation grabbed public interest and was seen as a major advance for medical technology.

Opposite: The Rolling Stones seemed in the mid-1960s to be the 'baddies' of pop; the flip-side to the Beatles' wholesome image. The Stones' image, fixed around the energetic sexuality of their leader Mick Jagger (b 1943), was confirmed for the press in 1967 when he was arrested on a drugs charge. Jagger (far right), however, like the other members of the group, looks wholesome enough in this early photograph; and their cult of 'evil' was to a large extent a matter of other people's successful marketing.

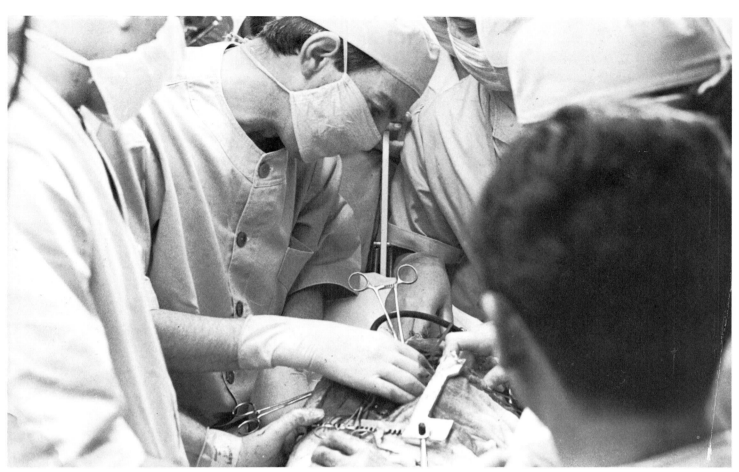

United States marines carried into action by helicopter during operation Double Eagle — a big American push designed to trap in a pincer thousands of Vietcong troops in central Vietnam. By late 1967 the massive American war effort had contained the Vietcong, but its costs and its social effects were beginning to arouse feelings of uncertainty and frustration within America.

Egyptian prisoners-of-war carrying a wounded comrade at a prison camp in Israel, June. These were casualties of the Six-Day War — 5 to 10 June — a 'preventive', highly-publicised war mounted by Israel against Egypt, Jordan and Syria — which led to the destruction of 400 Egyptian aircraft in one morning, and which inflicted an overwhelming and humiliating defeat on Egypt.

A British housewife takes a sub-machine gun with her as she walks with her children in the streets of Aden. Independence fighters had, since 1965, been conducting a harassing guerilla war against the British, who administered the Red Sea port as a colony within the South Arabian Federation of Arab Emirates. Britain withdrew from Aden in November, after 129 British servicemen had been killed.

The litter in the Paris streets left after more than ten thousand demonstrators had clashed with riot police, 24 May. The demonstrations were part of a wave of political unrest that swept through Europe and America that summer; the Paris riots were unique though, in that workers threw in their lot with the students during the violent street battles. At the height of the battles over 25,000 protestors fought 8,000 police.

A young Czech, arms raised in protest, faces Soviet tanks grinding through the streets of Bratislava in August. Under Alexander Dubcek (b 1921), the Czechs had begun a programme of liberalisation and limited reform — including relaxation of censorship — which alarmed the Soviet leadership. Russian forces numbering 200,000, with token contingents from East Germany, Hungary, Poland and Bulgaria, crossed the border into Czechoslovakia on 20/21 August. Those communist countries supporting Czechoslovakia — Rumania and Yugoslavia — were powerless to help.

Senator Robert Kennedy (1925-68) lies sprawled on the floor of a Los Angeles hotel, clutching a rosary and watched over by his wife, moments after being shot. He died next day, on 6 June. Kennedy had been his brother John's attorney general and had championed the civil rights movement; he had just begun his campaign for the Democratic presidential nomination.

Starving Biafran children wait for food at a refugee camp, July. Biafra, peopled by the Ibo tribe, seceded from Nigeria in May 1967; in response federal government troops entered Biafra. In the continuing civil war these children were the helpless victims — an estimated three million faced starvation in the war-stricken areas in the summer of 1968.

An anti-war demonstration outside the American embassy in London, October, protesting against the conviction of the American child-care expert Benjamin Spock — who had influenced the childhood of a generation — for advising young Americans to evade the draft for the Vietnam war. In the forefront is the British actress and activist Vanessa Redgrave (b 1937).

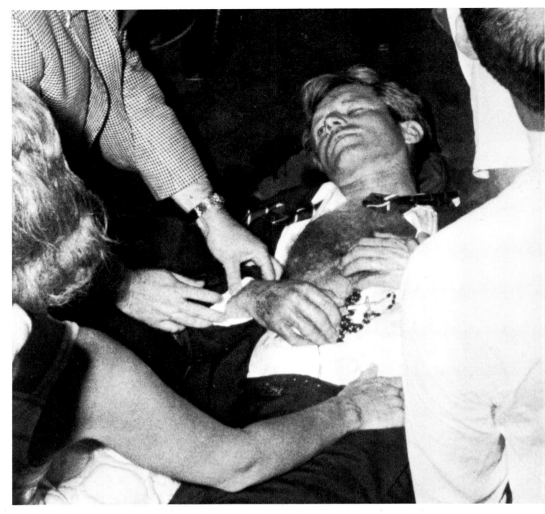

Man on the moon, 21 July: Colonel Edwin 'Buzz' Aldrin (b 1930), who set foot on the moon's surface eighteen minutes after Neil Armstrong (b 1931), salutes the American flag planted in the Sea of Tranquility. The landing as well as being a triumph for America and a dazzling victory in the space race was a triumph for technology and imagination. The landing was watched by millions on television the world over.

Queen Elizabeth II crowns her eldest son, Charles (b 1948), heir apparent to the throne, as Prince of Wales, at the investiture ceremony at Caernarvon Castle, 1 July. The prince's uniform, invented for the occasion, had been designed by his uncle, the Earl of Snowdon (b 1930).

Russian-born Golda Meir (1898-1978) became prime minister of Israel in February, after being a member of the Israeli cabinet continuously since 1949.

In Northern Ireland a three-day sectarian street battle in Londonderry followed a parade through the town by Protestant apprentice boys, 12 August. Here the camera catches a young boy — Molotov cocktail ready in his hand — wearing a World War II gas mask for protection against police tear gas.

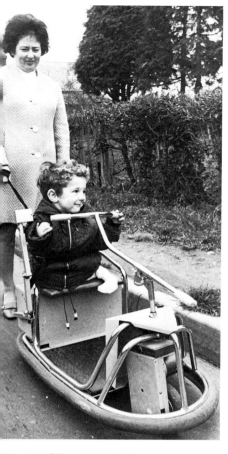

Five-year-old Ian Shorter of Kent was a thalidomide baby born with no legs and only one complete arm because his mother had taken pills containing thalidomide during her pregnancy. Thousands of babies throughout the world were born with similar deformities as a result of thalidomide; nearly 6,000 cases in West Germany alone. Parents sought compensation from the drug's manufacturer and, on 30 July, in a test case, damages were awarded to twenty-eight British thalidomide children and their parents.

Germaine Greer (b 1939), Australian lecturer in English at Warwick University. In 1970 her angrily polemic book *The Female Eunuch* exposed the sexual subservience of women to a male-dominated society. Like Marx's *Das Capital* in the previous century, Greer's book was more talked about than read; and more influential than first realised.

The British army advances up the Shankhill Road in Belfast, September. Ulster Catholic demands for equal political rights led first to protest marches, then to rioting until, in April 1969, the Ulster government asked for British troops to be sent in. By 1970 the army found itself beleaguered in the middle of sectarian violence.

For these children of an Israeli kibbutz on the border with Jordan, bedtime meant going together to their bomb, gas and rocket proof shelter for the night. Guerillas operating from within Jordan kept this and other border areas under continued harassing rocket and mortar attacks. One mother of the kibbutz told reporters proudly that the children 'learn to recognise the sound of the alarm siren almost before they recognise single words ...'

The moment when guerillas of the Palestine Liberation Organisation blew up a Boeing 707, one of four airliners they had hijacked and forced to fly to Dawson's Field in Jordan, in September. Terrorism was rapidly learning to feed off — and feed — television and the newspapers.

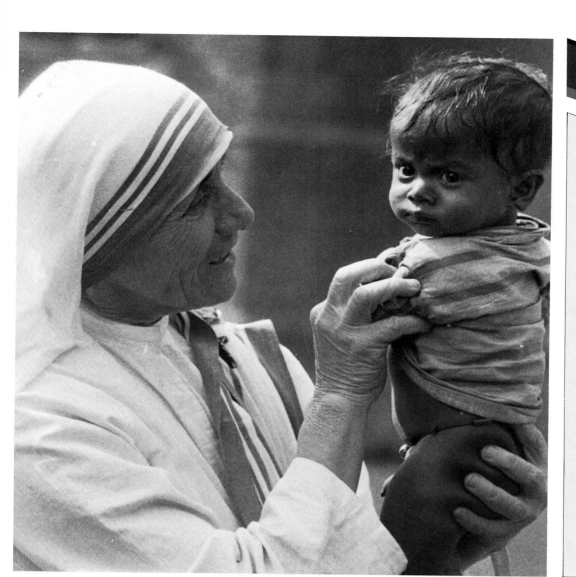

Mother Teresa (b 1910), the Albanian-born missionary — whose life is dedicated to helping the destitute and the sick in India and other deprived regions — was awarded the Pope John XXIII peace prize for 26 years' work with destitute street-dwellers and slum children in Calcutta. In 1979 she was awarded the Nobel Peace Prize for her work.

The Soviet Tupolev 144 supersonic airliner on public view at the Paris Air Show. Dubbed the 'Concordski' because it looked like the Anglo-French Concorde, the TU144 had on 31 December 1968, become the first supersonic airliner to fly, beating the Concorde prototype 001 by two months.

The vertiginous view over London from the Post Office Tower on 31 October, after an IRA bomb blasted a hole in its side thirty-one storeys up. Another bomb exploded near the Houses of Parliament and, as the Queen was to open parliament two days later, the normal ceremonial search of the parliamentary cellars in remembrance of Guy Fawkes was replaced by a more serious security check.

Opposite: A chauffeur leans on the bonnet of a Rolls Royce and reads of the bankruptcy of the company. Rolls Royce failed in 1971 not because of its car division but because of a disastrous contract to supply jet engines for a new American air liner. Nevertheless the collapse of a company that embodied all the virtues of reliability and quality shocked Britain. It also persuaded the then Conservative government to make a U-turn in policy, rescue Rolls Royce and begin to make huge sums of government money available to private industry.

Opposite: Pakistani soldiers guard the border with India, at a point just north of Calcutta where Indian and Pakistani gun batteries confronted each other from a distance of less than 75 yards. After a series of border disputes between the two countries, Pakistan mobilised its army in October. The Indo-Pakistan war began on 3 December, the day that India recognised the independence of Bangladesh, the breakaway state that had previously been East Pakistan.

United States president Richard Nixon (b 1913) is greeted by Mao Tse-tung on his arrival in China, February. Inevitably perhaps this was described in the press as an 'historic handshake', but it did in truth mark a new spirit of rapprochement between Nixon's America and Mao's China, which had been admitted into the United Nations only in the previous year.

British troops in the Northern Ireland town of Dungiven observe one minute's silence in memory of the thirteen civilians who had been killed in rioting in Londonderry two days earlier, on 30 January — another 'Bloody Sunday' — when soldiers opened fire on a banned demonstration parading in favour of a united Ireland. The Primate of All Ireland called for an enquiry. Two months after 'Bloody Sunday', the Northern Ireland parliament was closed and its power transferred to Westminster.

Opposite: An Arab terrorist talks to German police from a window in the Israeli Olympic team's quarters in the Olympic Village in Munich, 5 September. The Israeli team was held hostage by terrorists armed with grenades and machine guns in a siege that ended tragically in an airport shoot-out. Eleven Israeli athletes, five terrorists and a German policeman died. The Games were not abandoned.

1973

Princess Anne (b 1950), only daughter of Elizabeth II, leaving Westminster Abbey with Captain Mark Phillips after their wedding on 14 November. Much was made of this marriage — the bridegroom was the son of a rich businessman — as an example of the democratisation of the monarchy: the more cynical noted that it distracted from strikes and the international oil crisis caused in October by an Arab decision to ban the supply of oil to the USA, and to raise the price for crude oil by 70 percent.

An automatic camera in a San Francisco bank took this photograph of a woman taking part in an armed hold-up in May 1974. The woman was Patricia Hearst, daughter of an American millionaire newspaper publisher, who had been kidnapped eleven weeks before by an international terrorist group, the Symbionese Liberation Army. Her family had met a ransom demand that they should distribute two million dollars worth of food to the poor of San Francisco. But meanwhile Patricia Hearst had been turned to her captors' cause.

Russian writer Alexander Solzhenitsyn (b 1918) (left) arrives in Switzerland after being deported from the Soviet Union. His first novel, *One Day in the Life of Ivan Denisovich*, had been published in Russia with official permission in 1962, even though it revealed what life in the Russian prison camps was like. But his later novels were refused publication in Russia as he became increasingly critical of the Soviet system.

Previous page: There were explosions in London this year at the Boat Show, at Madame Tussaud's, at the Tower and, in June, at Westminster. Here the clockface of Big Ben is half hidden by smoke as a fireman fights the blaze in the 900-year-old Westminster Hall, where a bomb had left eleven people injured.

By July the long-running Watergate scandal was nearing its climax, and Nixon was within a month of resigning. Here, William Bittman (foreground), representing one of those involved in the burglary of the Democratic Party National Committee offices takes the stand. The burglars were charged with breaking in, photographing documents and planting surveillance equipment.

A woman and child run for cover to escape fighting in the streets of Nicosia, Cyprus. National Guard officers who favoured union with Greece launched a coup d'état against president Makarios (1913-1977), who fled the Island. A month later Turkey invaded and set up a Turkish state in the northern half of the island.

1975

With his queen beside him, Juan Carlos I (b 1938) addresses the Spanish parliament after taking the oath as king, 22 November. The grandson of Alfonso XIII (who fled Spain in 1931) Juan Carlos had been nominated in 1969 by Franco as his successor but soon shook off the Franco tag and led Spain back to parliamentary democracy, establishing free elections and granting an amnesty for political prisoners. Six years later, in February 1981, he faced and beat a threatened military coup by appearing on television to remind the forces of their duty to democracy.

Yasser Arafat (b 1929), chairman of the Palestine Liberation Organisation, addressing the United Nations General Assembly in November. Arafat had, in 1974, been recognised by Arab leaders as the 'sole legitimate representative of the Palestinian people'. He was the first person who was not a representative of a government ever to address the Assembly.

There had been no American combat troops in Vietnam since February 1973, but American advisors were still there when, in April, a North Vietnamese offensive finally overwhelmed the South Vietnamese army. Saigon fell on 30 April. The Americans mounted a massive airlift to take their own people back to the United States, but many pro-American Vietnamese were left behind to the mercy of the communists. Here desperate civilians try vainly to cling to one of the last, overloaded transport planes as it takes off. In neighbouring Cambodia — earlier in the same month — the communist Khmer Rouge army had driven the American-backed government from the capital, Phnom-Penh, and taken control of the country.

Opposite: Demonstrators in London's Trafalgar Square in June voicing their support for an Abortion Amendment Act intended to make it more difficult for women to get legal abortions.

Armed uniformed police cover two plainclothes detectives in a London street during the Balcombe Street Siege, in which a middle-aged couple, John and Sheila Matthews, were held hostage in their flat by four Irish Republican Army gunmen for nearly a week in December.

1976

The 'Cod War' between Britain and Iceland started in 1972, when Iceland unilaterally extended its fishing limits from 12 to 50 miles. The 'war' was marked by numerous, well-publicised incidents between Icelandic gun boats and Royal Navy ships sent to protect British vessels fishing in the disputed waters. Here, in one such confrontation, in January, the bows of the Icelandic gun boat *Thor* are embedded in the side of the frigate HMS *Andromeda*.

American sculptor Carl André's 'Low Sculpture' went on exhibition to an incredulous public in London's Tate Gallery in February; it was composed of some 120 firebricks. Although many supported the sculptor, there was a hysterical press outcry when it was found that the Tate had bought the work 'for an undisclosed amount' four years earlier.

Romania's brilliant gymnast Nadia Comaneci (here with her team-mate Theodora Ungureanu) became a popular international star at the 1976 Montreal Olympics. The Western press used words like 'elfin' to describe her and such was her impact that she was featured in a full-length American television programme, *Nadia — from Romania with Love*, a rare accolade for an athlete from behind the Iron Curtain.

Swedish Bjorn Borg (b 1956) playing in the men's singles finals at Wimbledon against Ilie Nastase of Romania. The two-hander Borg won in three sets. This was to be the first of his five consecutive Wimbledon singles titles. Borg retired in 1982, having proved himself arguably the world's all-time best tennis player. By the time he retired Borg had the kind of fame usually reserved for rock stars.

Perhaps because the West could offer no nationally approved outlet for aggression, the old profession of the mercenary soldier was revived in the 1970s, when numbers of mostly untrained and inexperienced youths took part in fighting in various parts of Africa. These men are some of the British survivors from a group of forty mercenaries who had fought in Zaire and were being returned, in some ignominy and with much publicity, to Britain in October.

1977

The new American president Jimmy Carter (b 1924) — who had, as governor of Georgia, declared that 'the time for racial discrimination is over' — appointed as United States ambassador to the United Nations a black politician, Andrew Young, here at Heathrow airport on his return from a meeting with African leaders in Khartoum, May 1977.

Punk — a basic form of rock music married to angry, often obscene words — became a cult during 1976 in deprived inner-city communities spreading later to more affluent areas. The deliberately offensive behaviour of many of the punk groups shocked older, conservative opinion. The British group shown here, the Sex Pistols, used obscenities in a television chat show — their 'punishment' was the cancellation of their recording contract and even greater fame among their followers. Their hit single *God Save The Queen* revealed a darker side to the Jubilee celebrations in Britain.

Queen Elizabeth II had in 1977 been on the throne for twenty-five years and there were civic and national celebrations to mark her Jubilee. Although the Queen was said to have 'mingled with her people as never before', traditionalism triumphed and there was still a noticeable distancing of monarch from subjects on most occasions. Here the Queen goes walkabout among a line of children at Deptford in East London.

In Minneapolis a fire-gutted warehouse is turned into a palace of icicles as tons of water from firemen's hoses freeze in a temperature of −29°C.

The Central African Republic became overnight the Central African Empire when, on 4 December 1976, its president Jean Bokassa, who modelled himself on Napoleon, declared himself emperor with tacit French approval.

President Anwar al Sadat (1918-1981) of Egypt addressing the Israeli parliament in November. In an unprecedented step, Sadat flew to Jerusalem to begin peace negotiations with Israel in the face of hostility from the rest of the Arab world. Israeli premier Menachem Begin (b 1913) made a return trip to Cairo the following month. Both men shared the Nobel Peace Prize in 1978 for these efforts to bring peace to the Middle East. Sadat was murdered by soldiers from his own army four years later; they had never forgiven him his attempt to make peace with Israel.

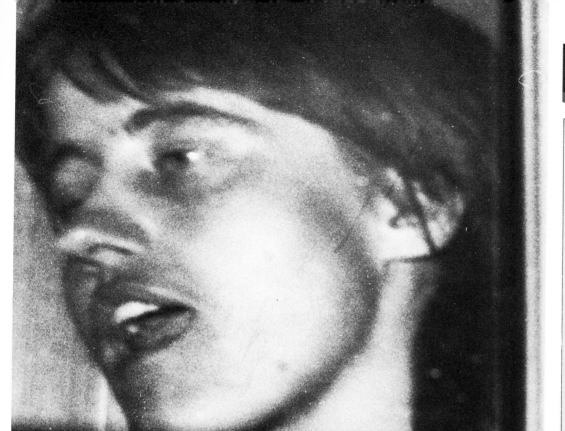

Wanted German terrorist Astrid Proll, a member of the Baeder-Meinhof Group, was found in September 1978 working in a London garage. The German authorities who wanted her extradited charged that the anti-capitalist, anti-American group she belonged to was responsible for six murders, over fifty attempted murders as well as bombings and bank raids.

Two leaders of the Rhodesian Patriotic Front — Robert Mugabe (b 1924) (left) and Joshua Nkomo (b 1917) — addressing a press conference in London in May after making known to the British foreign secretary their objections to Ian Smith's proposals for black majority rule in Rhodesia by the end of the year.

In Guyana in November horrified investigators arriving at the Jamestown 'commune of the People's Temple' found that adult members of the cult had committed mass suicide having first poisoned their children; bodies lay strewn around the old galvanised bucket from which they had each taken a cyanide-laced drink. Those who had refused had been shot. Above the 'throne' of their leader Jim Jones was a sign reading, 'Those who do not remember the past are condemned to repeat it.'

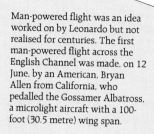

Man-powered flight was an idea worked on by Leonardo but not realised for centuries. The first man-powered flight across the English Channel was made, on 12 June, by an American, Bryan Allen from California, who pedalled the Gossamer Albatross, a microlight aircraft with a 100-foot (30.5 metre) wing span.

Karol Wojtyla, Archbishop of Krakow, Poland, became the first non-Italian pope for 450 years when — as John Paul II — he succeeded in October 1978 the previous pope, John Paul I, who had reigned for only 33 days. Pope John Paul II quickly showed himself to be a tireless traveller. He made the first-ever papal visit to Ireland in the autumn of 1979 and some 400,000 people assembled for his blessing when he went to the shrine at the small town of Knock. The Pope did not cross the border into the North.

A fortnight after the Shah had flown into exile, Ayatollah Ruhollah Khomeini (b 1900) stepped from the Air France plane that brought him back to Iran on 1 February, after sixteen years of exile. He returned to Iran as leader of the Islamic Revolution — initially with western backing — after the deposition of the Shah. After appointing a new government the Ayatollah retired to a theological seminary — but he remained *éminence grise* of the revolution, supporting the seizure of the United States embassy and its personnel in Tehran in November, and treating the war against Iraq as a relentlessly pursued religious crusade.

One of the many small boats that set out on a six-hundred mile journey across the South China Sea with refugees fleeing from the communist regime in Vietnam in 1979. The plight and sufferings of these Boat People — who were frequently savagely attacked by pirates — aroused enormous humanitarian concern in the West and most Western countries took in a quota of refugees. Over 250,000 are believed drowned in the exodus.

1980

Nuns file from the cathedral in San Salvador after the funeral of the murdered campaigner for civil rights, Archbishop Oscar Romero, 30 March. While a service was conducted in the cathedral a gun battle raged in the streets outside, during which forty people were killed and a hundred injured.

A Soviet convoy photographed on the outskirts of Kabul, the Afghan capital, halted at the scene of a sniper ambush in which two Russian soldiers have been killed. The Russians invaded Afghanistan at Christmas 1979 and by 1 January the Soviet army had nearly 40,000 troops in their occupying force: *Pravda* claimed that the Russian troops had been invited in.

An attempt in April to rescue the American hostages in Tehran, who were now in their sixth month of captivity, ended in disaster when helicopters of the American task force collided in the desert. The mission was aborted, but eight American soldiers died during the evacuation. The failure was held against President Jimmy Carter and was an element in his defeat in the 1980 presidential elections.

A hostage scrambles to freedom from the Iranian embassy in London after SAS commandos had stormed the building, 5 May. Armed men had seized the embassy on 30 April, taking everyone in the building hostage and threatening to blow up the embassy if their demands were not met. The SAS moved in to put a violent end to the siege after two of the hostages had been shot; only one of the gunmen in the embassy survived the attack.

Mount Saint Helens in Washington State erupts on 18 May, sending a cloud of steam and ash some 60,000 feet (18,000 metres) into the air. The explosion allowed scientists the chance to monitor the effect of debris in the atmosphere.

Lech Walesa (b 1943) chaired by his fellow workers at the Lenin shipyard at Gdansk, 30 August, after negotiating with the Polish government the right of workers to form independent unions and to strike. Walesa assumed the leadership of the Polish trade-union movement Solidarity, which was recognised by the Polish government in November but banned in the following year, when the Polish reforms went the same way as the Hungarian reforms of 1956 and those of Czechoslovakia in 1968.

British athlete Sebastian Coe winning the 1500 metres race at the 1980 Moscow Olympics in a world record time of 3 mins 32.03 seconds. East Germany's Jurgen Straub (right) was second and another Briton, Steve Ovett, third. The 1980 Olympics were boycotted by several countries, including the United States, Japan and West Germany, in protest against the Soviet invasion of Afghanistan.

Prince Charles announced his engagement to Lady Diana Spencer on 24 February. In June Lady Diana appeared at Ascot for Ladies' Day. She was married the following month in a service watched by a world-wide television audience of over 700 million.

The scene, outside Washington's Hilton hotel, of the attempted assassination of Ronald Reagan (b 1911) after the injured president has been bundled into his car to go to hospital, 30 March. On the right, agents pin the assailant, John Hinckley, against the wall; others tend to a wounded policeman and to the presidential press secretary, James Brady.

Firemen deal with the aftermath of the Brixton riots, April. The year 1981 was a year of rioting in Britain's run-down inner cities. Brixton's weekend of violence was followed in July by more riots, at Southall, Toxteth, Wood Green, Brixton again and Manchester.

The American space shuttle *Columbia* is successfully launched from Cape Canaveral on 7 August. It was to be the world's first re-usable space craft, landing like an airplane after each mission. A sister shuttle *Challenger*'s destruction in 1986, in front of the cameras seventy-two seconds after take-off shocked the world but didn't halt the space race. Within a month, both Russia and America had confirmed projected missions to Mars.

A scene from the National Theatre's production of *Romans in Britain*. In March 1982 the play's director, Michael Bogdanov, was privately prosecuted at the Old Bailey by Mary Whitehouse, President of the National Viewers and Listeners Association, for 'gross indecencies' enacted on stage during performances of the play — in one scene a British captive was homosexually raped. Support for the prosecution reflected a move away from the artistic freedom prevalent in the 1970s.

PLO leader Yasser Arafat says farewell to a Palestinian boy fighter before he leaves the city of Beirut. In June the Israeli army invaded Lebanon, aiming to drive out guerillas of the Palestine Liberation Organisation who operated from Arab refugee camps in the country. The Israelis surrounded the capital, Beirut, and insisted that PLO forces left the city. The evacuation of some 15,000 PLO fighters was eventually completed within a few days, at the end of August 1985. In September 1982 unidentified 'Christian militia' occupied the Sabra/Chatila area of Beirut and raped, tortured and massacred an unknown number of refugees running into thousands.

Opposite: Children's clothes, toys and balloons threaded into the wire around an American base in Britain. By 1982 it was known that the British Conservative government would permit United States' Cruise missiles to be deployed in Britain. In protest, peace camps — the best known being that at Greenham Common near Newbury (here) — were set up at some of the bases where the Cruise missiles were, in autumn 1983, to be installed. In June, over 200,000 people attended an anti-Cruise demonstration in London, and similar reactions took place in Holland and West Germany.

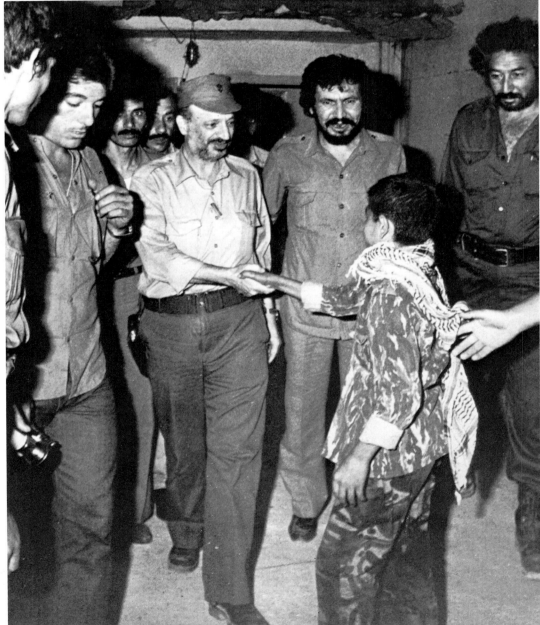

The hull of Henry VIII's famous warship *Mary Rose*, raised from the bed of the Solent where it had rested since it was wrecked in 1545, is lowered in its specially constructed cradle on to the barge that is to take it to Portsmouth. The wreck revealed much information about naval life in the sixteenth century.

An Argentine sailor in a lifeboat took this photograph of the old Argentine cruiser *General Belgrano* listing heavily as it begins to sink after being torpedoed by a British submarine, 2 May, during the Falklands crisis. There was much international controversy over the British action.

On 2 April, Argentine troops had invaded and captured the Falkland Islands, which the Argentines call the Malvinas and claim as their own. Britain despatched a Task Force and retook the Falkland Islands from Argentina after three and a half weeks of land fighting. In the conflict 255 British and 720 Argentinian lives were lost. This cross marks the grave of Colonel H. Jones, who was awarded a posthumous Victoria Cross for his bravery during the battle for Goose Green and Darwin; the grave overlooks Ajax Bay, through which many ships of the Task Force sailed.

Two relaxed American paratroopers 'chatting with a local resident' on the West Indian island of Grenada. The United States invaded Grenada, an independent state within the British Commonwealth, on 25 October after its premier, Maurice Bishop, had been shot and his People's Revolutionary Government replaced by a more left-wing regime. The United States' invasion contravened both international law and the United Nations charter — but was supported by many other West Indian countries.

December 1983 was a tense time for shoppers in London as the Irish Republican Army was conducting one of its periodic bomb campaigns in the capital. The first explosion was at an army barracks in Woolwich; then on 17 December a bomb was set off outside Harrods, London's most famous store, killing six people and injuring many more. Although the store was seriously damaged, it remained open for business.

Opposite: The chief editor of the West German magazine *Stern* holds up books that were claimed to contain the personal diaries of Adolph Hitler. The magazine, in what would have been the scoop of the century, was to begin publishing extracts from the diary in April, but on 6 May the German government — correctly as it turned out — pronounced them to be a forgery.

A mother and child picked out by the camera from the huge crowd of refugees at Korem Camp, Ethiopia. As though severe drought and growing famine were not enough, civil war added to the appalling sufferings of the Ethiopian people.

Policemen's helmets and a policewoman's hat still lie in the street outside the Libyan Peoples' Bureau in London five days after shooting from inside the building had wounded several Libyan demonstrators and killed WPC Yvonne Fletcher. The Bureau was besieged by the police and Britain broke off diplomatic relations with Libya. The siege ended on 27 April in the exchange of thirty Libyans from the Bureau with the British ambassador and other diplomats from the British embassy in Tripoli.

Opposite: The first man to have his own individual freedom of space was American astronaut Bruce McCandless, who on 7 February made, from the space shuttle *Challenger*, an 'untethered EVA with MMU' — extra-vehicular activity (with no umbilical cord connecting him to the shuttle or its life-support system) using a manned manoeuvring unit. Here, with earth far below him, he floats quite unconnected 320 feet (97.5 metres) from the shuttle.

India's new prime minister, Rajiv Gandhi (b 1944) watches over the cremation pyre of his mother, and predecessor as prime minister, Indira Gandhi (1917-1984). Mrs Gandhi was assassinated by two Sikh members of her bodyguard on 31 October, four months after she ordered her troops to storm the Sikhs' most sacred shrine, the Golden Temple at Amritsar.

In March Britain's National Coal Board announced its intention to close a number of pits that could not, in NCB terms, be mined economically. The miners' strike that immediately resulted became an increasingly bitter fight between the NCB and the National Union of Miners, the former backed tacitly by the government: the latter by, among others, miner's wives and women's groups who to an extent not seen before in an industrial dispute, organised themselves to support the strikers. These members of a women's support group are at a fund-raising fête in South Yorkshire, Summer 1984.

The women's 3000-metres race at the Los Angeles Olympics ended in disaster for two leading international athletes — American record-holder Mary Decker and the runner nominated by the press as her greatest rival, South African-born Zola Budd, competing for Britain. Seconds after this photograph was taken the two runners collided; Decker was sent sprawling off the track and Budd (leading here) was disqualified. The race was won, and the Olympic record broken, by a Romanian runner.

An injured soccer fan is carried to safety, 29 May, after supporters go on the rampage at the Heysel Stadium in Brussels before the start of the European Cup Final match between Liverpool and the Italian team Juventus. A stand wall collapsed under pressure from the crowd, leaving thirty-eight people dead and over 400 injured. English soccer teams were banned from Europe after this.

In South Africa throughout 1985 unrest continued, especially in the black townships. Here, on 9 July, in the township of Kwa-Thema a South Africa Broadcasting Corporation car is burned by mourners-turned-rioters at the funeral of four blacks killed by the police.

Irish pop singer Bob Geldof leads fellow pop singers in the finale of the *Live Aid* concert he inspired and organised in aid of African famine relief, 13 July. Advertised as 'the greatest gig in the galaxy', the spectacular show, at London's Wembley Stadium and JFK Stadium, Philadelphia, was watched by an audience of hundreds of thousands of fans and, through television, by billions of people — of all nationalities, religions and political creeds — throughout the world: over £60,000,000 was raised for aid and famine relief, and Geldof was nominated for the 1986 Nobel Peace Prize. It was undoubtedly the world's most successful example of the power to influence of television, radio, film and newspapers.

The space shuttle *Challenger* explodes seventy-two seconds after lift off, in the worst disaster in American space history, 28 January 1986. The crew of seven — including teacher Christa McAuliffe — were killed. Televised pictures of the explosion stunned America then the world; in Moscow the state radio station broadcast American music (Glenn Miller) in tribute. The development of the spacecraft/airplane cost almost $10,000,000,000 from the project's start in January 1972 to the first space shuttle flight by *Columbia* between 7 and 14 August 1981. The program was expected to run to as many as five shuttles, each one to have a life of about a hundred missions. And the success of *Columbia* — after nearly six years of no American manned flights — and the massive boost in confidence it gave to American expectation of the 'spacerace' explain in part, the trauma of *Challenger's* destruction. But although the shuttle program was badly disrupted and enquiries ordered, the spacerace itself was not halted. Within a month both Russia and America had confirmed their intention to go ahead with projected missions to Mars.

INDEX
MAJOR EVENTS AND CHARACTERS
Numbers in *italic* refer to illustrations

Abu Simbel *140*
Abyssinia, Italian invasion of *71*
Afghanistan, Soviet invasion of *174, 176*
Afrika Korps *88*
Airships *44, 59, 60, 67, 76*
Alamein, battle of *92*
Aldrin, Colonel 'Buzz' *147*
Alexandra, Tsarina *19, 36*
Alfonso XIII, King *17, 22, 63, 160*
Altitude, world record (1932) *65*
Amundsen, Roald *26, 28*
Ancre, battle of *37*
Antarctica, exploration of *14, 26, 27, 28, 124*
Anzac Cove, Gallipoli *34*
Arafat, Yasser *160, 180*
Arctic crossing, 1st under ice *123*
Armistice, WWI *42*
Asanuma, Injiro, assassination *129*
Astaire, Fred *70*
Astor, Nancy *44*
Astronaut, 1st woman *134*
Attlee, Clement *112*
Australia, 1st flight & back *53* 1st solo flight, woman *62*
Austrian civil war *70*

Balcombe Street siege *162*
Balfour, Arthur *44*
Bannister, Roger *116*
Barnard, Dr Christiaan *142*
Battle of Britain *85*
Beatles, the *141*
Beatty, Sir David *33*
Berlin blockade *105*
Berlin Wall, building the *131*
Blériot, Louis *20*
Blitz, the *88, 89, 90, 97*
Blucher, sinking of *33*
Boat people, the *173*
Bogart, Humphrey *104*
Bokassa, Jean, coronation *168*
Borg, Bjorn *165*
Brixton riots, London *178*
Budd, Zola *188*
Buddhist priest, immolation *135*

Campbell, Sir Malcolm *67*
Cassino, battle of Monte *96*
Challenger, space shuttle *179, 187, 191*
Chaplin, Charlie *45*
Charles, Prince of Wales *147*
Chiang Kai-shek *56, 98*
Chinese civil war *56, 75*
Churchill, Sir Winston *24, 34, 45, 80, 93, 95, 112*
Clay, Cassius *138*
Clemenceau, Georges *44*
Cobham, Sir Alan *54*
Coe, Sebastian *176*
Coelacanth, discovery of *112*
Columbia, space shuttle *179*

Comaneci, Nadia *164*
Compiègne, railway carriage *42*
Cuban missile crisis *133*
Cultural revolution, Chinese *140*
Czechoslovakia, Soviet invasion of *145*

Dalai Lama, flight of *127*
Dali, Salvador *116*
Dean, James *118*
Decker, Mary *188*
Dempsey, Jack *55*
Depression, the *45, 58, 60, 61, 66, 69, 70, 74, 82*
Derby, suffragette death at *30*
De Valéra, Éamonn *49*
Diana, Princess of Wales *177*
Dior, Christian *109*
Dogger Bank, battle of *33*
Dollfuss, Chancellor *70*
Dreadnoughts, race to build, WWI, *30, 45*

Easter rising, the *35*
Eden, Anthony *112*
Edward VII, King *11, 19, 22*
Edward VIII, King *73, 77*
Einstein, Albert *57*
El Salvador, civil war in *174*
Elizabeth II, Queen *112, 115, 147, 167*
Everest, conquest of *115*

Falklands crisis *182, 183*
Finnish-Russian war *81, 84*
Flemming, Alexander *95*
Flight, development of *13, 20, 54, 56, 61*
Flyer I *13*
Foch, Marshal Ferdinand *42*
Francis Ferdinand, Archduke, assassination *32*
Fuchs, Sir Vivian *124*

Gable, Clark *82*
Gallipoli *34*
Gandhi, Mahatma *62, 64*
Garbo, Greta *55*
Geldof, Bob *190*
General Belgrano, sinking of *182*
General strike, British *54*
George V, King *22, 25, 30, 39*
German Rhineland, French occupation *47*
Goebbels, Joseph *71*
Goering, Herman *102*
Greenham Common *181*
Greer, Germaine *149*
Grenada, US invasion *184*

Haley, Bill *121*
Harrods, London, bombing *184*
Hess, Rudolf *102*
Heysel Stadium, riot at *189*

Hillary, Sir Edmund *115, 124*
Hindenburg, Paul von *68*
Hindenburg, crash of *76*
Hitler, Adolf *52, 68, 77, 86, 87, 98*
Hungarian rising, the *120*

Inchon, landing at *109*
India, independence *62, 103*
Indo-China, French in *114*
Indo-Pakistan war *153*
Iranian revolution *172, 175*
Iranian embassy, siege *175*
Ireland, Northern, conflict *148, 149, 154*
Irish Republican Army *45, 49, 152, 162, 184*
Iwo Jima, raising US flag *99*

Jagger, Mick *143*
Jarrow march, the *74*
Jewish immigrant ship, interception *103*
John Paul II, Pope *171*
Johnson, Amy *62*
Juan Carlos I, King *160*
Jutland, battle of *36*

Kelly, Grace *119*
Kennedy, John F *130, 133, 136, 138,* assassination *136*
Kennedy, Robert, assassination *146*
Khomeini, Ayatollah Ruhollah *173*
Korean war *108, 109, 110*
Krushchev, Nikita *125, 130, 133*
Kuomintang *56, 98, 107*

Land speed record (1933) *67*
Landru, Henri *46*
Laos, civil war *137*
Leaky, Louis *132*
Lebanon, Israeli occupation *180*
Leigh, Vivien *82*
Libyan Peoples' Bureau, London, siege *186*
Lindbergh, Charles *56*
Liston, Sonny *138*
Liveaid concert *190*
Lloyd George, David *22, 48*
London WWII, bombing of *88, 89, 90, 97*
Louis, Joe *111*

MacArthur, Douglas *109*
Madrid, bombing of *72* fall of *81*
Manners, Muriel *20*
Mao Tse-tung *75, 98, 140, 154*
Marciano, Rocky *111*
Marconi, Guglielmo *10, 29*
Mary Rose, raising *182*
Mau Mau uprising *113, 117*
Meir, Golda *147*
Mile, 4-minute *116*
Miners' strike, British *188*

Montgomery, Bernard *88, 92, 100*
Moon landing *147*
Mount St Helens, eruption *175*
Mountbatten, Earl *103*
Mugabe, Robert *169*
Munich agreement, the *78*
Mussolini, Benito *48, 52, 78*

Nagasaki, bombing of *101*
Nautilus, nuclear powered submarine *123*
Nehru, Jawaharlal *103*
Nicholas II, Tsar *19, 39*
Nixon, Richard *154, 159*
Nkomo, Joshua *169*
Nobel prize, literature (1907) *18* peace (1978) *168* (1979) *151,* physics (1909) *10,* (1921) *57*
Nuremberg trials *102*
Nureyev, Rudolf *132*

Olympic games, 1908 (London) *19,* 1936 (Berlin) *74,* 1948 (London) *106,* 1972 (Munich) *155,* 1978 (Montreal) *164,* 1980 (Moscow) *176,* 1984 (Los Angeles) *188*
Olympic village, siege *155*
Oswald, Lee Harvey, assassination *136*
Owens, Jesse *74*

Palestine Liberation Organisation *150, 160, 180*
Panama Canal, opening *32*
Paris riots *145*
Pearl Harbor, attack on *90*
Peoples' Temple, suicide *170*
Piccard, Auguste *65, 114*
Pietri, Dorando *19*
Post Office tower, explosion *152*
Prohibition *46, 59*

Rainer III, Prince *119*
Rasputin, Grigory *36*
Reagan, Ronald, assassination attempt *177*
Richthofen, Manfred von *42*
R IOI, crash *60*
Rogers, Ginger *70*
Rolling Stones, the *143*
Rome, march on *48*
Rommel, Erwin *88*
Roosevelt, Franklin D *93, 95, 105*
Ruby, Jack *136*
Ruhr, French occupation *50*
Russian revolution *39, 41*
Russo-Finnish war *81, 84*
Russo-German armistice, WWI *41*
Russo-Japanese war *14, 15*

Saar plebiscite *118*
Sadat, Anwar al *168*

'Saint Valentine's day massacre,' *59*
San Francisco earthquake *17*
Sarajevo, assassination at *32*
Sex Pistols, the *166*
'Sharpville massacre' *128*
Sidney Street, siege of *24*
Sino-Japanese war *144*
Solidarity, Polish trade union *176*
Solzhenitsyn, Alexander *157*
Somme, battle of *37*
South Pole, race for *26, 27, 28*
Space shuttle *179, 187, 191*
Space walk, 1st untethered *187*
Spanish civil war *72, 76, 78, 81*
Stalin, Joseph *95*
Sudetenland, annexation of *78*
Suez crisis *119*
Suffragette movement *20, 24, 30, 40, 44, 53*
Sydney Harbour bridge, opening *65*

Teheran conference *95*
Teresa, Mother *151*
Tereshkova, Valentina *134*
Thalidomide children *149*
Thoma, General von *92*
Titanic 29
Tokyo earthquake *50*
Tollund man *108*
Tolstoy, Leo *15*
Transantarctic expedition *124*
Trieste, bathyscaphe *114*
Truman, Harry S *105*
Tunney, Gene *55*
Tz'u Hi, Empress *13*

Unemployment *see* Depression

VE day, London *100*
Versailles, treaty of *44, 47*
Vietnam, American involvement *138, 142, 144, 161,* protest *142, 146*
Vietnam, South, fall of *2, 161, 173*

Walesa, Lech *176*
Wall Street crash *58, 60*
Warsaw uprising *93*
Watergate *159*
Weimar republic, inflation *50*
Western front, the *37, 38, 42*
Westminster, bombing *158*
Wilhelm II, Kaiser *22, 30*
World War I *12, 24, 30, 32, 33-43*
World War II *72, 80, 82-101*
Wright brothers *13*

Ypres, battle of *41*

Zaire, independence *131*
Zog, King *82*